SUCCESS at WORK

Globe
Fearon

Upper Saddle River,
New Jersey

Lead Editor: Rosely Himmelstein
Project Manager: Stephanie Cahill
Production Editor: Angela Dion
Marketing Manager: Katie Kehoe
Designers: Janice Noto-Helmers, Sharon Scannell
Electronic Publishing Specialist: Phyllis Rosinsky

Reviewers:
Patricia Ellen Berdan., M.A., B.A.
Resource Specialist
Will Rogers Middle School
Fair Oaks, CA

Evy Friend, M.A., B.A.
Program Specialist. Florida Department of Education
Tallahassee, FL

Paul R.Gallaher, M.A., B.A.
Program Specialist, Florida Department of Education
Tallahassee, FL

Cindy Forrester Gilbert, M.A., B.A.
Member of Alabama Special Education Task Force Committee
Birmingham, AL

Phyllis Klemstein M.S., B.S.
Teacher
Holmes High School
San Antonio, TX

Jane Hulme, B.S.
Teacher
Mission Middle School
Belleuve, NE

Carrie Donaldson. B.A.
Teacher
Madison School
Madison, TN

ISBN 0-130-23323-4

Printed in the United States of America

2 3 4 5 6 7 8 9 10   04 03 02 01 00

SUCCESS at WORK

Table of Contents

A Note to the Student

Congratulations! You have reached an important new stage in your life. You are ready to get a job.

Until now, other people usually told you what they expected from you. Your family told you what to do at home. Your teachers let you know what to do at school.

Things are different now. You will be making most of your own decisions. Your life from now on will be based mainly on choices you make for yourself.

In **Success at Work**, you will read about people who also decided to go to work. They are thinking about the things that you will be thinking about. Here are the people you will read about in this book:

This is Anita.
She thinks about what kind of job would be right for her.

This is Terrence.
He thinks about the steps to take to find a job.

This is Ashley.
She thinks about what it means to be a good worker.

This is Manuel.
He thinks about what people at work do to understand each other.

This is Ling.
She thinks about how people at work get along with one another.

This is Dennis.
He thinks about how to keep up with changes on a job.

This is Tanya.
After some good experience at work, she thinks about moving on to a better job.

All of these people are setting out to get jobs. They want to do them well. They are making new decisions and learning new skills. The text and the activities in this book will make it possible for you to do the same.

You will learn how you, too, can have success at work.

Unit 1
Looking at Life

LUNCHTIME IN THE SCHOOL CAFETERIA

It was lunchtime, and the school cafeteria was crowded. Anita sat down next to her friend Steve.

"Hi," said Steve. "What's going on?"

"Well," answered Anita, "I've decided that after graduation in June I'm going to get a full-time job."

Steve waited to hear more.

Anita continued. "I'm a little worried. The only job I ever had was baby-sitting for my neighbor's kid. I hope I can handle a real job. And I hope it's something I'll enjoy."

Anita has to think about her future. She wants a job. She wants to do well. She needs to think about what she is good at doing. She has to decide what kind of job is right for her.

What Do You Think?

What kind of things are you good at doing? What jobs might be right for you?

Deciding to get a job is a big step. In this unit, you will learn about:

- Defining Success
- Knowing Yourself
- Setting Goals

LESSON 1
DEFINING SUCCESS

Lesson Objective

This lesson will help you to answer this question:

- **What is success?**

Words to Know:

goal   something that you want and try to work toward
success   doing what you set out to do

Thinking About the Future

Anita will be graduating soon. She thinks about what she wants for the future. She must now set some new goals for herself. A **goal** is something that you want and try to work toward. Anita wants to earn money to pay for her clothes and food. She wants to be able to take care of herself as much as possible.

After thinking about what she wants, Anita writes down her goals on a piece of paper.

> ### GOALS
> – I want to get a job I enjoy.
> – I want to do my job well.
> – I want to use or learn the skills I will need to do the job.
> – I want to be proud of myself for doing a good job.

When she reaches her goals, Anita will have **success**. Success is doing what you set out to do.

Anita has to think about how to reach her goals. If she wants success, she has to be sure to set goals that are right for her. She has to think about the kind of person she is and the kind of work she would like to do. She also has to figure out what things she does best. Before you set goals, you need to know which ones are right for you. In Lesson 2, you will learn about "Knowing Yourself."

Checkpoint

What is success?

Think about your answer to this question. Write your answer on a separate piece of paper. Discuss your ideas with a partner. Then share these ideas with the class.

WORKPLACE PRACTICE

This activity will give you a chance to think about successes that you already have had in your life.

JOB TIP

Sometimes it takes more than one try to have success.

> **A. On a separate piece of paper, write your answers to the questions below.**
>
> 1. Have you ever had a job—at home, at school, or outside of school?
>
> 2. Did you have success at the job? Explain.
>
> 3. If you had success, how did you feel?
>
> 4. If you did not have success, what could you have done better?
>
> **B. Form a small group with other classmates.**
>
> Take turns sharing your answers.
>
> **C. Have a class discussion.**

LESSON REVIEW

Key Words

Draw a line from the word to its correct definition.

1. goal   a) doing what you set out to do

2. success   b) something that you want and try to work toward

Thinking About Defining Success

If you agree with the sentence, put a check mark next to the sentence.

3. _____ Success is having what other people have.

4. _____ Success is reaching the goals you set for yourself.

Workplace Workshop

5. Have a discussion with people at home. Ask about a person who set out to do something—and did it. Tell your class about this person. Discuss this question: Why was this person a success?

LESSON 2
KNOWING YOURSELF

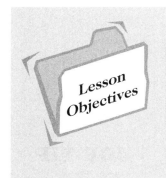
This lesson will help you to answer these questions:

- **Why is it important to know yourself when you are thinking about a job?**
- **What are some things you should know about yourself?**

Words to Know:

personality   all of a person's habits, behavior, and other qualities
abilities   skills or talents for doing something

Everyone is Different

Like Anita, you have a lot to think about when you consider getting a job. You have to think about the kind of job that's best for your **personality**.

You are different from everyone else. Your personality is different from anyone else's personality. Your personality is all your habits, behavior, and other qualities.

You also have to think about your **abilities**. Your abilities are your skills and talents. You want a job that requires you to do the things that you do best.

When you know about yourself, you can choose a job that's right for you. And when you choose a job that's right for you, you have a good chance to reach your goals.

Anita thinks about what she likes to do. She likes styling hair, reading, and talking on the telephone.

Checkpoint

Why is it important to know about yourself when you are thinking about getting a job?

Think about your answer to this question. Write your answer on a separate piece of paper. Discuss your ideas with a partner. Then share these ideas with the class.

Knowing Who You Are

The more you know about yourself, the more you will be able to make smart decisions about your future. Knowing yourself will help you get the job that's best for you. To know yourself means:

- to know what kind of person you are
- to know what you like to do
- to know what you don't like to do
- to know the kind of place you would like to work

You can answer the questionnaire below to learn about yourself.

JOB TIP

Talk to your family and friends about what you enjoy doing. They may help you think about what your interests are.

Know Yourself Questionnaire

Check Yes or No for each question.

	YES	NO
Think about what kind of person you are:		
Do you work best with others?	☐	☐
Do you work better on your own?	☐	☐
Are you shy?	☐	☐
Do you enjoy helping people?	☐	☐
Think about what you like and don't like:		
Do you like to work with your hands?	☐	☐
Do you like any hobbies or activities?	☐	☐
Are there certain things you like to do in your free time?	☐	☐
Are there any tasks that you don't like to do?	☐	☐
Think about the place you would like to work:		
Would you like to work outdoors?	☐	☐
Would you like to work indoors?	☐	☐
Would you like to work in a quiet place?	☐	☐
Would you like a job that takes you from place to place?	☐	☐

What are three things you should know about yourself?

Think about your answer to this question. Write your answer on a separate piece of paper. Discuss your ideas with a partner. Then share these ideas with the class.

Checkpoint

WORKPLACE PRACTICE

This activity will help you learn about your personality and your interests. It will help you choose the job that's right for you.

A. Write your answers to the following questions on the lines.

1. Have you had a paid or unpaid job that you enjoyed? What was it?

   _____

2. What activities after school do you enjoy most?

   _____

3. Do you like to work alone or on a team? Why?

   _____

4. Have you ever worked at a job or task where the time passed quickly? What was it?

   _____

B. Work with a partner.

Check the places that sound interesting to you. Then compare your list with your partner's list. Tell each other why you checked certain items.

_____ a kitchen	_____ a vehicle (train, bus, ship, plane, car)
_____ a store	_____ a farm
_____ a carpentry shop	_____ a school
_____ a garage	_____ a hospital
_____ an office	_____ a hotel

C. Work with a partner.

Think about working with people. Would you like

- to work alone?
- to work with children or young people?
- to work with older people or senior citizens?
- to work with sick or disabled people?
- to work with a mix of different kinds of people?

You and your partner can explain your choices to one another.

LESSON REVIEW

Key Words and Ideas

Complete each sentence with a word from the box.

personality	abilities

1. Sheila has a nice _____ . She will make a good waitress.

2. Jonas believed that his _____ to build and paint furniture made him the right person for the carpentry job.

Write the answer to the following question on the line.

3. What should you know about yourself when you're thinking about a job?

_____

Thinking About Knowing Yourself

Circle the letter of the correct answer.

4. Josie loves animals. She also likes to stay busy all day. The best job for her may be:

   a) to wrap packages.

   b) to work in a hair salon.

   c) to answer phones in an animal hospital.

5. The right person for a job as a helper in a day-care center would be:

   a) someone who liked to work with children.

   b) a person who liked a place that was always quiet.

   c) a person who needed everything to be neat all the time.

Workplace Workshop

6. Walk in your community with your classmates. Make a list of jobs that you see people doing. In class, write the name of each job on a slip of paper. Put all the slips in a bag. Take turns pulling out a slip of paper and reading it. State why the job is or is not a good match for you. Help each other with your lists.

LESSON 3
SETTING GOALS

This lesson will help you to answer these questions:

- **Why is it important to set goals?**
- **How can you set goals that you can reach?**

Words to Know:

long-term goal	a goal that can be met in several months or a year
short-term goal	a goal that can be met in several hours, days, or weeks
realistic	within your reach

A Direction for Your Life

Goals are important. Goals help you get what you want in your life. To reach a goal, you need to make decisions that bring you closer to it. Anita's **long-term goal** is to take care of herself as much as possible. A long-term goal is a goal that can be met in several months or a year.

Anita must make decisions that will help her reach her goal. She must set some **short-term** goals. A short-term goal is a goal that can be met in several hours, days, or weeks. Finding a job is one of Anita's short-term goals.

Setting a long-term goal is like planning a trip. It is a place you want to reach in your life. When you plan a trip, you have to think about how to get there. Short-term goals are the steps you take to make sure you reach the place you plan to go.

Anita's long-term goal is to take care of herself. She hopes to be able to buy her own food.

Why is it important to set goals?

Think about your answer to the question. Write your answer on a separate piece of paper. Discuss your ideas with a partner. Then present your ideas to the class.

Set Goals That You Will Be Able to Reach

When you set your goals, you want to know that you can reach them. You want to be sure that if you work hard, you will be successful.

To be sure that you will reach your goals, you need to set goals that are realistic for you. When a goal is **realistic**, it means that it is a goal that is within your reach. It means that you can really do the things that are necessary to reach your goal. You know that you will be able to carry out your plan.

Here are some things to think about when you are setting your goals:

- Remember that your goal is for you. Someone else may set a different goal—one that is right for that person. Your goal should be right for you.

- Trust yourself. Listen to your "gut" feelings about what seems right for you.

- One of your goals at this time is to get a job. Think about what kind of job you might want. Think about the education or experience or training that you may need. Ask yourself the questions below.

SOME HELPFUL QUESTIONS

— What do you need to know to do the job?

— Do you know enough now to do the job?

— What training do you need to do a good job?

— Is it possible for you to get training?

— Do you have the time to get the training?

It's Not Always Easy

Sometimes it may seem easier to set goals for someone else. Make sure your goals are your own. Why is it a mistake to try to reach another person's goals?

If you want a job and you want to do well, you need to be aware of what you can do. You want your plan to become real—not just a dream. You want to set goals that you can reach.

How can you set goals that you can reach?

Think about your answer to the question. Write your answer on a separate piece of paper. Discuss your answer with a partner. Then write your ideas down and read them to the class.

Checkpoint

LESSON 3 • 9

WORKPLACE PRACTICE

This activity will give you practice at setting goals.

A. Write your answers to the following questions on the lines.

1. Do you have a goal for tomorrow? What is that short-term goal?

_____

_____

_____

2. Do you have a goal for next week? What is that short-term goal?

_____

_____

_____

3. Do you have a goal for next year? What is that long-term goal?

_____

_____

_____

B. Choose a partner. With your partner, list four jobs that sound interesting to you.

Job 1: _____

Job 2: _____

Job 3: _____

Job 4: _____

C. With your partner, list some possible short-term goals for each job.

for Job 1: _____

_____

for Job 2: _____

_____

for Job 3: _____

_____

for Job 4: _____

_____

LESSON REVIEW

Key Words and Ideas

Complete each sentence with a word from the box.

short-term goal   realistic   long-term goal

1. Vera's plan or _____ is to volunteer in a community center's kitchen this summer. Her long-term goal is to work in a restaurant after graduating.

2. Shira's goal is to be a bus driver. It is a _____ plan only if she learns how to drive.

3. Carlos likes to fix the things, so his _____ is to be a school custodian someday.

Write the answer to the following question on the lines.

4. Why should your goals be realistic?

   _____

   _____

Thinking About Setting Goals

5. Jennifer's long-term goal is to be a word processor in an office. A good short-term goal for her would be to:

   a) learn how to play the piano

   b) take a science course in school

   c) learn how to type

6. Hilda has decided to volunteer at a nursing home. What do you think her long-term goal is?

   a) to work in a senior citizens' center

   b) to be a farmer

   c) to travel

Workplace Workshop

7. With a small group of classmates, think of people in your community who have jobs that are interesting. Together, prepare a list of questions to interview these people. Each member of the group interviews one person. Read the interviews afterward to the group, or role-play the interviews with partners.

Unit 1 Review
L o o k i n g   a t   L i f e

In this unit you learned about:

- **Defining Success**   • **Setting Goals**
- **Knowing Yourself**

I. Vocabulary

Write the letter of the correct definition next to each word.

____ 1. success

____ 2. realistic

____ 3. goal

____ 4. personality

____ 5. short-term goal

____ 6. abilities

____ 7. long-term goal

a) a goal that can be met in several hours, days, or weeks

b) a goal that can be met in several months or a year

c) skills or talents for doing something

d) doing what you set out to do

e) within your reach

f) something that you want and try to work toward

g) all of a person's habits, behavior, and other qualities

II. Main Idea

Circle the letter of the correct answer.

8. When you think about getting a job, an important question to ask is:

   a) Is the job right for my personality and abilities?

   b) Is it a job that my friends want?

   c) Are other people good at this job?

9. You will be able to make smart decisions about your future when you:

   a) see that your friends have made the right decisions.

   b) know yourself as much as possible.

   c) make decisions that your friends think are good.

10. When a person does what he or she sets out to do:

    a) that person is a success.

    b) the person has reached his or her goal.

    c) both a and b are correct answers.

III. What Would You Do?

Write your answers to the following questions on the lines.

11. You have decided to get a job. What are two things you should start thinking about?

   _____

   _____

12. You are a person who likes to work with numbers. What kinds of jobs would be good for you?

   _____

   _____

13. Your long-term goal is to work in a restaurant kitchen. What would be a good short-term goal?

   _____

14. Walter likes to be outdoors as much as possible. He is thinking about two jobs. One job is with a messenger service. The other job is with a photo lab. When he asks you for your advice, what do you say?

   _____

   _____

15. Your brother wants to know the difference between a long-term goal and a short-term goal. What do you tell him?

   _____

   _____

16. You like to work with people. You also like movies. A job in a video store could be right for you. Your best friend Tony is a housepainter. He wants you to get a job with his company. What do you say to him?

   _____

   _____

17. Charlene is thinking about two jobs—one is with a carpenter's shop and the other is in a camera store. Charlene gets sick around sawdust. Which job should she take—and why?

   _____

   _____

IV. Solving Workplace Problems

18. You are a manager in a flower shop. You need to hire someone to work in the store. Two people apply for the job. One is Carrie. She likes gardening in her backyard at home. Tim comes for an interview too. He would like a job that takes him from place to place. Who would you most likely hire for the job? Explain your answer.

_____

_____

19. If Tim asked you for advice, what would you tell him?

_____

_____

_____

20. If you needed someone to deliver flowers, who would you hire? Explain.

_____

_____

V. Unit Replay

Go back to the story on page 1. Reread it. Ask yourself again: What kind of things are you good at doing? What jobs might be right for you? Write your answer on the lines.

_____

_____

_____

VI. You . . . and Looking at Life

**Check ✔ the boxes next to the questions you can answer now.
Write an ✘ next to the ones you think you need to work on more.**

   ☐ What is success? (Lesson 1)

   ☐ Why is it important to know yourself when you are thinking about a job? (Lesson 2)

   ☐ What are some things you should know about yourself? (Lesson 2)

   ☐ Why is it important to set goals? (Lesson 3)

   ☐ How can you set goals that you can reach? (Lesson 3)

If you put an ✘ next to any question, go back and review the lesson.

Unit 2
Getting a Job

PEOPLE ON THE WAY TO WORK

At 8:00 in the morning, traffic was very heavy. People were on their way to work. Some people were on their way to office buildings. Some were going to their jobs in restaurants. Others were headed for stores. Perhaps they sold clothing, or car parts, or greeting cards. Terrence watched them as he walked to school.

Terrence was graduating from high school in a few months. Soon he would need a job too. He had spent a lot of time thinking about what kind of job would be right for him. Terrence decided that he wanted to work in a hospital. He enjoyed taking care of people.

Finding a job would be the next step. Terrence wondered how all the people around him got their jobs.

What Do You Think?

What steps might you take to find a job?

Finding a job takes a little time. In this unit, you will learn about:

- Looking for Work
- Using Want Ads
- Applying for a Job
- Going on an Interview
- Following Up
- Starting a Job

LESSON 4
LOOKING FOR WORK

Lesson Objectives

This lesson will help you answer the following questions:

- **Where can you get information about jobs?**
- **Where should you look to find a job?**

Words to Know:

resources	people and places that have useful information
networking	talking to people about jobs
want ads	advertisements placed by people who have jobs to fill
employment agency	a place that has listings of job openings

How to Get Information About Jobs

Terrence thought about what **resources** could help him find a job in a hospital. Resources are people and places that have useful information. Terrence spoke to his neighbor, Mr. Lee, who was a nurse in a hospital. Mr. Lee brought Terrence to the hospital to talk to people about jobs. Talking to people about jobs is called **networking**.

Mr. Lee introduced Terrence to other people who worked at the hospital.

Next, Terrence looked at **want ads** in a newspaper and magazines. Want ads are advertisements placed by people who have jobs to fill. He looked up all the jobs he could find about working in a hospital. Then Terrence went to the library. The librarian told him about the library's bulletin board and about other bulletin boards in the community.

Checkpoint

Where can you get information about jobs?

Think about your answer to this question. Write your answers on a separate piece of paper. Discuss your answer with a partner. Then share your ideas with the class.

Where to Look for a Job

There are many places you can look for a job. There are many different resources you can use to help you with your search. Think about the resources you could use. You can use networking, **employment agencies**, want ads, and the Internet. (You will learn more about the Internet in Lesson 32.) Employment agencies are places that have listings of job openings.

Here are some tips about using these resources.

JOB TIP

Your community center may have bulletin boards that list job opportunities.

⭐ Job Resources ⭐

Networking

- Ask relatives and people you know about job openings.
- Meet with job counselors and teachers at your school. Sometimes they have job listings.
- Try to meet people who work in places you might like to work.

Employment Agencies

- Make a list of all local employment agencies.
- Set up a time to go in and talk to a counselor.
- Explain what kind of job you want.
- Tell about any job experience you have.
- Act politely and dress neatly.

Want Ads

- Look in newspapers, magazines, or check bulletin boards. Libraries and supermarkets are two places that often have bulletin boards.
- Choose jobs that match your skills.
- Cut out the ads that interest you and tape them to a sheet of paper.

Using the Internet

- Find Web sites that list jobs.
- Enter key words to find jobs that interest you.
- Print out or save information that will be useful.

Where do you look to find a job?

Think about your answer to this question. Write your answer on a separate piece of paper. Discuss your ideas with a partner. Make a poster for the class that shows where to look for jobs.

Checkpoint

This activity will give you practice at looking for a job.

A. **Think about some people and places in your community that might help you find a job. Write them on the lines. Keep in mind the kind of job you want as you choose your resources.**

Resource 1:

_____

Resource 2:

_____

Resource 3:

_____

B. **Now work with two friends and brainstorm some more resources with them. It might be names of people who already have the kind of job you want. It might be a news magazine that has want ads. It might even be a new Web site of job listings.**

Person:

_____

Magazine:

_____

Newspaper:

_____

Web site:

_____

Agency:

_____

Resource:

_____

C. **Now choose your top two resources and write them on the lines below. Keep this list handy as you read the rest of the Unit.**

Resource 1:

_____

Resource 2:

_____

LESSON REVIEW

Key Words and Ideas

Complete each sentence with a word from the box.

| networking   want ads   resources   employment agency |

1. Joan knew three people who might be good _____ in her job search.

2. Terrence turned to the _____ listed in the newspaper.

3. Terrence found that _____ — or talking to different people—helped him learn about jobs.

4. At the _____, Manny learned about several job openings.

Write the answer to the following question on the line.

5. How can employment agencies help you find a job?

   _____

   _____

6. How can networking help you find a job?

   _____

   _____

Thinking About Looking for Work

Circle the letter of the correct answer.

7. Which of the following is **not** a resource?

   a) a family member

   b) a want ad

   c) a pencil

   d) a magazine

Workplace Workshop

8. Look in the Yellow Pages under "Employment Agencies." Write down a list of agencies in your town or city.

It's Not Always Easy

Looking for a job sometimes seems like hard work. But try to keep a good attitude! How can a good attitude make people want to help you?

LESSON 5
USING WANT ADS

This lesson will help you answer these questions:

- **What do want ads tell you about jobs?**
- **What do you need to know to understand want ads?**

Words to Know:

alphabetical order	when items are listed in order of the letters of the alphabet: (a, b, c)
abbreviation	a written word or phrase with several letters left out

Where to Find Ads for Jobs

Mrs. Bates was the school's job counselor. She showed Terrence how to use want ads. She explained that you can find want ads in newspapers, magazines, bulletin boards, and even on the Internet.

In a local newspaper, Mrs. Bates pointed to column headings that were in heavy print. These headings broke the sections up into job types. In their paper, hospital jobs were under the heading "Health Care." In other papers, they might appear under different headings—for example, "Medical Workers" or "Hospital Workers."

The want ad that Terrence liked was listed under "Health Care."

Terrence noticed that one of the ads listed the job title, the address to write to, how much the job paid, and which skills were needed for the job. Another simply listed the title of the job and a phone number. Many asked for a résumé. You will learn about résumés in the next lesson.

What do want ads tell you about jobs?

Think about your answer to this question. Write your answer on a separate piece of paper. Talk over your ideas with a partner. Then make a list.

Reading Want Ads

Keep in mind the following tips as you look through the want ads for a job:

- Want ads usually are listed in **alphabetical order**. This is when items appear in the order of the letters of the alphabet. For example, **a**ircraft cleaner comes before **b**ellhop, which comes before **c**abdriver, and so on.

- Circle the ads that interest you.

- Note who you should contact.

- People who place want ads often leave out letters from many of the words they use. A written word or phrase with several letters left out is called an **abbreviation**.

Here are some common abbreviations that you will find in want ads.

COMMON ABBREVIATIONS IN WANT ADS

exper.	experience
req'd	required
corp.	corporation
attn.	attention (the person to write to)
hr.	hour
wk.	week
yrs.	years
H.S. stdnt.	high school student
w/gd skills	with good skills
P/T	part-time
F/T	full-time
asst.	assistant
lic.	license
nec.	necessary
trnees.	trainees
oppty.	opportunity
mgr.	manager
co.	company
bet.	between
wpm	words per minute (refers to typing speed)

It's Not Always Easy

At first, looking at all the want ads can be confusing. Before you begin to read them, make a list of possible jobs that interest you. Why is it a good idea to narrow your search?

What do you need to know to understand want ads?

Think about your answer to this question. Write your answer on a separate piece of paper. Talk over your ideas with a partner. Then share them with the rest of the class.

Checkpoint

WORKPLACE PRACTICE

This activity will give you practice using want ads to find a job.

A. **Think about a job you would like to have. Then work with a partner to find three want ads for that job. You can use the listings from a local newspaper. Decide which ad is the best one for you and answer the following questions about it. Use a separate piece of paper if you want to do more than one. (You may need to contact the company for information that is not in the ad.)**

1. What is the title of the job?

   _____

2. What salary does the job pay?

   _____

3. What skills does the job require?

   _____

4. What education does the job require?

   _____

5. Is the job full-time or part-time?

   _____

6. What other information is in the ad for the job?

   _____

B. **Now answer the following questions:**

7. Why is this job right for you?

   _____

   _____

8. Why are you right for this job?

   _____

   _____

C. **Talk to your partner about your job choice.**

LESSON REVIEW

Key Words and Ideas

Complete each sentence with a word from the box.

abbreviation	alphabetical order

1. We say a list is in ———————————————— when the items are listed by order of letters.

2. An ———————————— is a shortened form of a word or phrase.

This is the want ad under "Health Care" that Terrence answered. Read it and answer the questions that follow.

Nurse's Aides

Several openings. No exper. Will train. 35 hr. wk. Salary to start: $10,000–$12,000. Send résumé: Lincoln General Hospital, 14 Greene St., Chicago, IL 60691

3. How much experience does the job require?

   a) some   b) none   c) 35 hours

4. How many hours a week is a person expected to work?

   a) 14   b) 10   c) 35

Thinking About Using Want Ads

Circle the letter of the correct answer.

5. Which list of jobs is in alphabetical order?

   a) mechanic, nurse, doctor   c) doctor, mechanic, nurse

   b) nurse, mechanic, doctor

Workplace Workshop

6. Copy the information from five want ads that you find in a newspaper. Then work in small groups to identify the kind of information in each ad. Next, create a bulletin-board display that describes the different information that is found in the want ads.

LESSON 6
APPLYING FOR A JOB

This lesson will help you answer these questions:

- **What is a résumé and why do you need one?**
- **What are the parts of a résumé?**

Words to Know:

résumé	a summary of your education and work experience
employer	the person or company who hires workers
cover letter	a letter that is sent with a résumé to introduce you to an employer
references	people who know you well and will tell others you are a good worker

What Is a Résumé?

Terrence chose to answer an ad that asked for a **résumé**. Terrence asked his job counselor what a résumé was and why he needed one. Mrs. Bates said, "A résumé is a summary of a person's education and work experience. Your résumé will tell an **employer** if you are right for the job." An employer is a person or company that hires workers.

Mrs. Bates explained that a résumé would help the hospital find out if Terrence was the best person for the job. She said, "You should put information in a résumé that tells about your skills and experience." You will read Terrence's résumé on the next page.

Cover Letters

When you send a résumé, you also need to include a **cover letter**. A cover letter is a letter that you send with your résumé, introducing yourself to the employer. The first paragraph tells which job you want. It explains how you found out about it. The first paragraph of Terrence's letter said:

> I would like to apply for the position of nurse's aide. I saw your ad in Sunday's **Glover Times**.

The second paragraph gives details about why you are the person for the job. The last paragraph tells what you are including with your letter, such as a résumé. End the cover letter by asking for an interview. Remember to sign your letter.

What is a résumé and why do you need one?

Think about your answer to this question. Write your answer on a separate piece of paper. Now talk about your ideas with a partner. Then share your ideas with the class.

The Basic Parts of a Résumé

Here is the résumé that Terrence prepared.

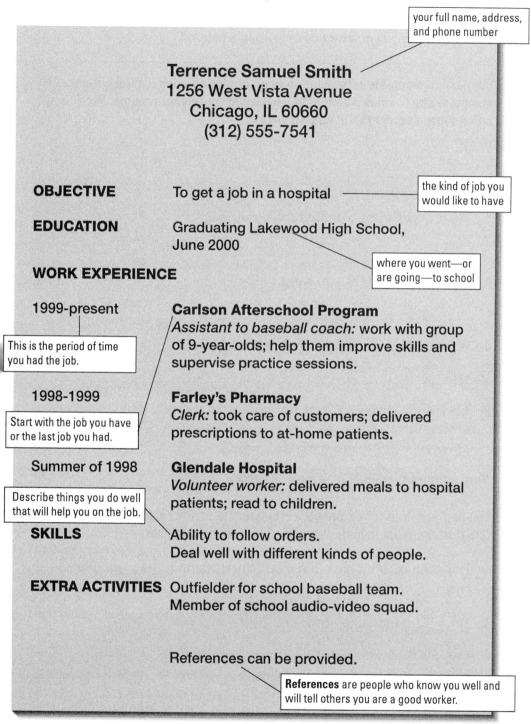

Terrence Samuel Smith
1256 West Vista Avenue
Chicago, IL 60660
(312) 555-7541

> your full name, address, and phone number

OBJECTIVE To get a job in a hospital

> the kind of job you would like to have

EDUCATION Graduating Lakewood High School, June 2000

> where you went—or are going—to school

WORK EXPERIENCE

1999-present

> This is the period of time you had the job.

Carlson Afterschool Program
Assistant to baseball coach: work with group of 9-year-olds; help them improve skills and supervise practice sessions.

1998-1999

> Start with the job you have or the last job you had.

Farley's Pharmacy
Clerk: took care of customers; delivered prescriptions to at-home patients.

Summer of 1998

> Describe things you do well that will help you on the job.

Glendale Hospital
Volunteer worker: delivered meals to hospital patients; read to children.

SKILLS Ability to follow orders.
Deal well with different kinds of people.

EXTRA ACTIVITIES Outfielder for school baseball team.
Member of school audio-video squad.

References can be provided.

> **References** are people who know you well and will tell others you are a good worker.

JOB TIP

If you want to use people as references, call them first. Ask if it is okay to use their names.

What are the parts of a résumé?

Think about your answer to this question. Write your answer on a separate piece of paper. With a partner, make a list of the parts of a résumé. Then read your list to the class.

Checkpoint

WORKPLACE PRACTICE

This activity will give you practice in writing a résumé.

A. Suppose that you are interested in applying for a job as a salesperson at a computer store. Think about how you would write your résumé. Work with a partner to answer the questions below.

1. What would you put at the top of the résumé?

   _____

2. What experience would you include?

   _____

3. Which skills would you want to list?

   _____

4. What else should you include in the résumé?

   _____

5. What should you write at the bottom of the résumé?

   _____

B. Now write your résumé on a separate piece of paper.

C. You and your partner exchange résumés with another pair of students. Use this checklist to make sure each résumé is complete.

6. Does the résumé have a name, address, and phone number?

   ❏ YES   ❏ NO

7. Does it include experience?

   ❏ YES   ❏ NO

8. Does it include the person's skills?

   ❏ YES   ❏ NO

9. Does it have the person's education?

   ❏ YES   ❏ NO

10. Does it mention that references are available?

   ❏ YES   ❏ NO

LESSON REVIEW

Key Words and Ideas

Draw a line from the word to its correct definition.

1. cover letter

2. employer

3. résumé

4. references

a) people who will tell others about you

b) a letter sent with a résumé

c) a person or company that hires workers

d) a summary of a person's education and work experience

Circle the letter of the correct answer.

5. The main purpose of a résumé is to show an employer

   a) where you live.

   b) that you are right for the job.

   c) your family history.

Thinking About Applying for a Job

Write the answers to the following questions on the lines.

6. Carol and Stan have applied for the same job. Carol sends a résumé, Stan does not. Who do you think has a better chance of getting an interview? Explain your answer.

   _____

   _____

7. Why should you think carefully about who to include in the reference part of your résumé?

   _____

8. Why should you send a cover letter with a résumé?

   _____

   _____

Workplace Workshop

9. Invite people in your family or community to share their résumés with you. Post the résumés on the class bulletin board. Take turns indicating the basic parts of the résumés.

It's Not Always Easy

Sometimes it's hard to decide what to put in your résumé. Include only information that is useful. Why is it important to make your résumé clear and to the point?

LESSON 7
GOING FOR AN INTERVIEW

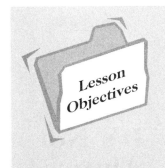

Lesson Objectives

This lesson will help you answer these questions:

- **How can you do well in an interview?**
- **Which questions should you be prepared to answer?**

Words to Know:

first impression	what someone thinks about you after meeting you
salary	the amount of money a job pays
benefits	extras offered by an employer, such as health insurance, vacation time, education plans, and retirement plans

A Good Interview

At his interview, Terrance made a good **first impression.** A first impression is what someone thinks about you after meeting you.

Terrence was sure that his interview went well.

When you go on an interview, keep the following things in mind:

- Be on time and dress correctly.
- Shake hands with the person who is going to interview you.
- Talk about your skills. Explain how they will help you.
- Prepare a list of questions about the job.
- Look the interviewer in the eye when you talk.
- Thank the interviewer for his or her time.

Checkpoint

How can you do well in an interview?

Think about your answer to this question. Write your answer on a separate piece of paper. Discuss your thoughts with a partner. Then share your ideas with the class.

Questions You May Be Asked in an Interview

Try to think of the types of questions you might be asked in a job interview. Always answer in a positive way. Read some of the questions Terrence was asked during his interview, as well as his answers.

Terrence's Interview

Interviewer: Tell me something about yourself.

Terrence: **I'm 18 years old. I'm a senior in high school, and I'm looking for a full-time job.**

Interviewer: What makes you interested in working in a hospital?

Terrence: **I like helping people. I enjoy working in a busy place.**

Interviewer: How much do you expect to be paid?

Terrence: **The ad said that the beginning salary was in the range of $10,000 to $12,000. That's about what I'm looking for—to start.**

Interviewer: How can you help us here at Lincoln General Hospital?

Terrence: **I took a science lab course in school and I know how to handle a lot of the instruments. I've also worked with patients during a summer job so I'm used to dealing with people in a hospital.**

Interviewer: What are some of your hobbies?

Terrence: **I enjoy baseball very much. In fact, I'm coaching my kid brother's team. I also like to hike and go fishing.**

JOB TIP

Never say bad things about another employer or work experience. Even if you have had a bad experience, find something good to say about it.

Talking About Salary and Benefits

The money that you will make is important. However, you do not want people to think that **salary** is the most important part of the job. The salary is the amount of money a job pays. Show that you are also interested in the experience.

An interview is a time to talk about **benefits**. Benefits are extras offered by an employer. Benefits may include health insurance, vacation time, and sick leave. Part-time workers often do not get the same benefits as full-time workers. Ask questions to make sure you understand which benefits are being offered to you.

What questions should you be prepared to answer?

Think about your answer to this question. Write your answer on a separate piece of paper. Discuss your ideas with a partner. Then make a list of questions and read them to the class.

Checkpoint

WORKPLACE PRACTICE

This activity will give you practice for going for an interview.

A. Suppose you have an interview for a job as an assistant in an office. You want to do your best to prepare for the interview by practicing answers to questions you think may be asked. Take turns with a partner to answer the questions below.

1. Describe your work experience.

_____

_____

_____

2. What skills would you bring to the job?

_____

_____

3. What did you enjoy the most during school?

_____

4. What are some of your strengths? What are some of your weaknesses?

_____

_____

B. Complete the following two activities and then role-play an interview with a partner.

5. List other questions you think an employer might ask you.

_____

_____

6. Write two questions you might want to ask the employer about the job.

_____

_____

_____

LESSON REVIEW

Key Words and Ideas

Complete each sentence with a word from the box.

first impression	salary	benefits

1. Vacation time and health insurance are types of _____.

2. It is important to make a good _____ during an interview.

3. A _____ is the amount of money a job pays.

Write the answer to the following question on the lines.

4. What are three things to remember when you go for an interview?

   _____

   _____

   _____

Thinking About Going for an Interview

Circle the letter of the correct answer.

5. Which of the following is a question you might ask during an interview?

   a) "What if I can't do the job?"

   b) "How much money do you make?"

   c) "Can you tell me about the benefits you offer?"

6. Which of the following is a good way to prepare for an interview?

   a) Make a list of questions about the job.

   b) Make sure to wear jeans and a T-shirt.

   c) Make a list of your favorite TV stars.

Workplace Workshop

7. With your classmates, brainstorm a list of questions an employer might ask during an interview for a job at a movie theater. Take turns providing possible answers to the questions. Write the questions and answers on a separate sheet of paper. Then discuss types of behavior that may not be right during an interview.

It's Not Always Easy

Most people feel nervous before an interview. Being prepared will make you more relaxed. Why is it important to prepare for an interview?

LESSON 8
FOLLOWING UP

This lesson will help you answer this question:

- **What should you do after an interview?**

Word to Know:

thank-you note   what you write to thank the person who interviewed you

Writing a Thank-You Note

Terrence really wanted the job in the hospital. His mom suggested that he write the interviewer a **thank-you note**. A thank-you note is what you write to thank the person who interviewed you. It also is a way to let the interviewer know that you are interested in the job. Read Terrence's note.

Ms. Janis McMurphy
Lincoln General Hospital
14 Greene Street
Chicago, IL 60691

August 8, 2000

Dear Ms. McMurphy,

It was great meeting with you last week. I liked learning about the position of nurse's aide. I know that I would like working with the patients. I hope that I will also be able to work with children. I really enjoy spending time with young people.

Thank you for taking the time to meet with me. I look forward to hearing from you.

Sincerely,

Terrence S. Smith

Making a Follow-Up Call

If you have not heard about the job after two weeks, give the company a call. Ask if the job has been filled. A phone call will show that you are still interested in the job. Companies often take some time to decide if they want to hire someone. You may even be called back for another interview.

What should you do after an interview?

Think about your answer to this question. Write your answer on a separate piece of paper. Discuss your ideas with a partner. Then share these ideas with the class.

WORKPLACE PRACTICE

This activity will help you practice writing a thank-you note.

Suppose that you have just finished an interview with Mr. Jim Flores at a record company. Work with a partner to write the thank-you note that you would send to Mr. Flores.

_____

_____

_____

_____

_____

LESSON REVIEW

Key Words

Circle the phrase in parentheses that correctly completes the sentence.

1. After an interview, write (a thank-you note, a résumé).

2. A thank-you note lets the interviewer know that
   (you are interested in the job, you will be on time for work).

Thinking About Following Up

Write the answers to the following questions on the lines.

3. Donna interviewed for a job as a bank teller. She has not heard from the bank in two weeks. What should she do?

   _____

4. Felix said "thank you" to the man who interviewed him. Should he also write a thank-you note? Explain your answer.

   _____

Workplace Workshop

5. Suppose that you are calling an employer to follow up on a job. Have a classmate play the role of the employer. Act out the conversation you might have.

It's Not Always Easy

You may not get the job you apply for. If so, talk to someone about it. Everyone has disappointments. Why is it important to share our experiences with others?

LESSON 9
STARTING A JOB

Lesson Objectives

This lesson will help you answer these questions:

- **How can you feel comfortable at a new job?**
- **What kind of forms might you have to fill out?**

Words to Know:

income tax	money that everyone who works pays to the government
withholdings	money that your employer takes from your paycheck for taxes
time sheet	a sheet that lists the number of hours worked

A New Job

On Friday afternoon, the hospital called Terrence. He got the job!

Terrence was thrilled to tell his mother the good news.

There is a lot to learn the first day on a new job. To get comfortable at a new workplace, here are some things to do:

- Meet the people you work with. Repeat their names when you are introduced. It's a good way to remember.

- If you are given an employee handbook, read it carefully.

- Find the location of the cafeteria and the supply closet.

- Let your boss know when you arrive. If you want to know something about your job or the company, ask your boss.

How can you feel comfortable at a new job?

Think about your answer to this question. Write your answer on a separate piece of paper. Discuss your ideas with a partner. Then share these ideas with the class.

Checkpoint

Filling Out Forms

One of the first things you will do when you get a job is to fill out a form for your **income tax.** Income tax is money that everyone who works pays to the government. Your income is the amount of money you earn. The income tax you pay to the government is based on the total amount of money you earned for the year.

By the end of the year, most of your income tax is already paid. Your employer holds back some money from each paycheck and sends it to the government. The money that is taken out of your paycheck and sent to the government is called **withholdings**.

You probably will have to fill out a **time sheet.** A time sheet lists the number of hours you worked for the week. Your salary will be based on the number of hours you write down.

Here is the time sheet Terrence filled out for his first week of work.

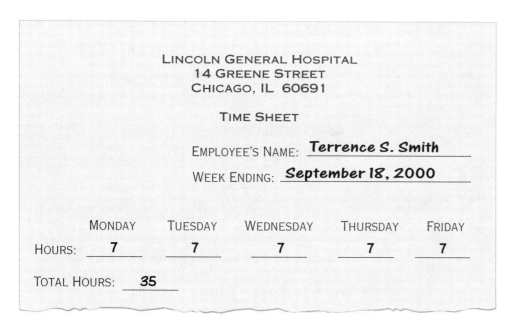

LINCOLN GENERAL HOSPITAL
14 GREENE STREET
CHICAGO, IL 60691

TIME SHEET

EMPLOYEE'S NAME: *Terrence S. Smith*

WEEK ENDING: *September 18, 2000*

	MONDAY	TUESDAY	WEDNESDAY	THURSDAY	FRIDAY
HOURS:	7	7	7	7	7

TOTAL HOURS: 35

It's Not Always Easy

Some forms may be confusing to fill out. Be sure to ask if you need help. Why should you stop filling out the form until you know how to do it?

Understanding Benefits

As you read in Lesson 7, benefits are insurance plans, education plans, and retirement plans offered by an employer. Not all jobs offer benefits. And different companies offer different kinds of benefits.

If you get a job that does offer benefits, you will be asked to fill out the necessary forms. If you do not understand something on a form, ask for help.

What kind of forms may I have to fill out?

Think about your answer to this question. Write your answer on a separate piece of paper. Discuss your ideas with a partner. Make a list of these ideas and read it to the class.

Checkpoint

This activity will help you understand how to fill out a time sheet.

Suppose you have just completed one week at your new job at the Apex Mitten Factory. In order to get paid, you need to fill out your time sheet.

A. Fill out the time sheet below. Some of the information has already been entered.

- Write your name.
- Enter the number of hours you worked each day. (This is already done.)
- Add up the number of hours you worked. Put that figure in the blank for "Total Hours."
- Multiply that figure by the hourly rate ($5.25 in this case).

The answer is the amount of money you earned. It is your Total Pay.

Apex Mitten Factory
Time Sheet

Name: _____

Week starting: __May 11, 2000_____

Week ending: __May 15, 2000_____

	Monday	Tuesday	Wednesday	Thursday	Friday
Hours:	7	7	7	7	7

Total Hours x Hourly Rate = Total Pay

_____ x __$5.25__ = $ _____

B. With a partner, answer the following questions.

1. What would you earn for the week if you worked 25 hours?

   _____

2. What would your week's salary be if you were paid $7.00 an hour?

   _____

LESSON REVIEW

Key Words and Ideas

Complete each sentence with a word from the box.

income tax	time sheet	withholdings

1. The _____ that Terrence pays the government is based on the amount of money he earns.

2. _____ is the money your employer takes from your paycheck for taxes.

3. Wendy had to fill out a _____ every two weeks in order to get paid.

Write your answers to the following questions on the lines.

4. Why is it important to read the employee handbook carefully?

    _____

5. Why is it important to fill out a time sheet carefully?

    _____

Thinking About Starting a Job

Circle the sentences that are true.

6. Withholdings is the money that your employer takes out of your paycheck for taxes.

7. All companies offer the same benefits.

8. The first day on a job is always easy.

9. It's a good idea to let your boss know when you have arrived at work.

Workplace Workshop

10. Suppose that today is your first day of work at Jackson's Diner. You are introduced to a another employee who has worked there for two years. Have a conversation with this person. Ask questions about your new workplace. Then change roles with your partner so you're the experienced worker.

JOB TIP

Before you get a job, you have to get a Social Security card. Look in the telephone book to find the Social Security office near you. Go there and apply for a card if you don't have one.

Unit 2 Review
Getting a Job

In this unit you learned about

- Looking for Work
- Using Want Ads
- Applying for a Job
- Going on an Interview
- Following Up
- Starting a Job

I. Vocabulary

Write the letter of the correct definition next to each word.

____ 1. resources	**a)**	a letter that is sent with a résumé to introduce you to an employer
____ 2. abbreviation	**b)**	the amount of money a job pays
____ 3. networking	**c)**	a written word or phrase with several letters left out
____ 4. income tax	**d)**	a place that has listings of job openings
____ 5. salary	**e)**	talking to people about jobs
____ 6. cover letter	**f)**	a summary of your education and work experience
____ 7. benefits	**h)**	extras offered by an employer
____ 8. résumé	**i)**	the money that everyone who works must pay the government
____ 9. employment agency	**j)**	people and places that provide useful information

Underline the word or phrase in parentheses that completes each sentence.

10. A (first impression, income tax) is what someone thinks about you after meeting you.

11. Advertisements placed by people who have jobs to fill are called (employment agencies, want ads).

12. A (cover letter, thank-you note) is what you write to a person after an interview.

13. When items are listed in order of the letters of the alphabet, they are in (alphabetical order, a time sheet).

14. The person or company who hires workers is an (abbreviation, employer).

15. You use (benefits, references) when you want people to tell others about you.

16. (Withholdings, résumés) is money that your employee takes from your paycheck for taxes.

17. A sheet that lists the number of hours worked is a (time sheet, cover letter).

II. Main Ideas

Circle the letter of the correct answer.

18. A résumé should always include your

    a) work experience.   **b)** hours.   **c)** income tax.

19. One thing NOT to do on an interview is to

    a) be well dressed.   **b)** chew gum.   **c)** ask questions.

III. What Would You Do?

Write your answer to the following questions on the lines.

20. You want to find a part-time job listed in the newspaper. Where in the newspaper would you look?

    _____

    _____

21. You are being considered for a job. The person who interviewed you wants a reference. What should you think about before giving out a reference?

    _____

    _____

22. You are interested in a part-time job. You would like to work in your local supermarket. In preparing your résumé, what will you write as your objective?

    _____

    _____

23. You are applying for a job as an aide in a day-care center. What questions do you think the interviewer might ask you?

    _____

    _____

IV. Solving Workplace Problems

Today is Marta's first day at her job at a music CD store. She is handed several forms to fill out. Marta isn't sure what to do with the time sheet.

24. Explain to Marta what this form is and how to fill it out.

_____

_____

_____

25. When Marta receives her paycheck, she notices that some money has been taken out. She asks you why this is so. What do you tell her?

_____

_____

_____

V. Unit Replay

Go back to the story on page 15. Reread it. Ask yourself again: What steps might you take to find a job? Write your answer on a separate sheet of paper.

VI. You . . . and Getting a Job

**Check ✔ the boxes next to the questions you can answer now.
Write an ✗ next to the ones you think you need to work on more.**

- ❑ Where can you get information about jobs? (Lesson 4)
- ❑ Where should you look to find a job? (Lesson 4)
- ❑ What do want ads tell you about jobs? (Lesson 5)
- ❑ What do you need to know to understand want ads? (Lesson 5)
- ❑ What is a résumé and why do you need one? (Lesson 6)
- ❑ What are the parts of a résumé? (Lesson 6)
- ❑ How can you do well in an interview? (Lesson 7)
- ❑ Which questions should you be prepared to answer? (Lesson 7)
- ❑ What should you do after an interview? (Lesson 8)
- ❑ How can you feel comfortable at a new job? (Lesson 9)
- ❑ What kind of forms may you have to fill out? (Lesson 9)

If you put an ✗ next to any question, go back and review the lesson.

Unit 3
Being a Good Worker

WORKING AT THE HOTEL STATLER

Ashley worked at the Hotel Statler. She was part of a large group. Many people were needed to run the hotel.

When Ashley got to work each day, she changed into her uniform. Then she went straight to the main office. There her boss would tell her the tasks for the day.

Ashley worked with the maintenance crew. She was one of the people who made sure that the rooms were neat and clean. She also checked to see that the rooms had everything the guests needed.

Were there enough fresh towels? Did all the lightbulbs work? Was there dust under the desk?

Ashley tried very hard to be a good worker.

What Do You Think?

What do you think it takes to be a good worker?

Good workers have to keep certain things in mind. In this unit, you will learn about:

- Dressing for Work
- Getting to Work on Time
- Understanding the "Big Picture"
- Following Instructions
- Managing Time
- Being Organized
- Being Responsible

LESSON 10
DRESSING FOR WORK

This lesson will help you answer these questions:

- **Why is it important to dress correctly for work?**
- **How can you be sure to wear the right clothes?**

Words to Know:

pride	feeling that you have importance
casual clothes	clothes worn when relaxing, such as around the house, at a picnic, or while playing
dress code	rules for what to wear in a certain place, such as a job or restaurant

The Importance of Dressing Correctly for Work

Ashley wears a uniform to work. All the people who work at the hotel have to wear uniforms. Ashley makes sure that her uniform is in good condition. It is important to the hotel and to Ashley that she is neat and clean. Looking good shows that Ashley's job is important to her. It shows that she has **pride** in her work.

Ashley checks her uniform for the next day.

Every evening, Ashley checks to see that her uniform is ready for the next day. Ashley feels good when she looks her best. It also makes her employers feel good. Dressing correctly shows that Ashley is serious about her job. It's good for business when people are serious about their jobs. Guests will keep coming back to the Hotel Statler.

Why is it important to dress correctly for work?

Think about your answer to this question. Write your answer on a separate piece of paper. Discuss your ideas with a partner. Then present your ideas to the class.

How to Choose What to Wear

Ashley wears a uniform so she doesn't have to think about what to wear each day.

Unlike Ashley, most people don't wear uniforms to work. They must choose clothes that are right for their jobs. Different jobs require different kinds of clothes. For some jobs, simple everyday clothes are fine. These are called **casual clothes**. Other jobs may require different kinds of clothing.

It's important to find out if the company has a **dress code** for work. A dress code is a set of rules that says what is right to wear in a certain place. If there is no dress code, ask yourself these questions:

- What do other workers wear?
- What kind of activities will I do while working?
- Will I be able to do my job in these clothes?
- What will be the most comfortable clothes to wear?
- What is the weather like? Is it hot or cold or rainy?
- Is the weather going to change?
- Will I be outdoors? Will I be indoors?
- Will I be on my feet a lot? What shoes feel best?

Here are suggestions to help you choose the right clothes for work:

—Don't wear clothes that are dirty, torn, or have missing buttons.

— Wear simple jewelry—for example, don't wear many chains or earrings.

— Wear clothes that will make it easy to do your job.

— Don't wear strong-smelling perfumes.

— Don't wear clothing with sayings or symbols.

— Wear casual clothes only if it is right for the job.

How can you be sure to wear the right clothes?

Think about your answer to this question. Write your answer on a separate piece of paper. Discuss your ideas with a partner and illustrate them in a poster.

Checkpoint

WORKPLACE PRACTICE

This activity will help you decide how to dress correctly for work.

Each column in the box is a list of clothes that would be right for a certain job.

A. Look at the chart below. Then read each job description that follows. On the line, write the number of the column that lists the right clothes for the job.

1	2	3	4	5
sneakers	swimsuit	jeans	old shirt	nice pants
hair net	large sun hat	sweatshirt	hat for sun	skirt/dress
uniform	T-shirt	gloves	sneakers	shirt & tie
apron	sunscreen	boots	dust mask	sweater
	sandals		painting pants	sports jacket
				nice shoes

1. You are raking leaves in Mr. Brown's backyard in the late fall.

   _____

2. It is summer, and you are sanding and painting houses outdoors.

   _____

3. You are a word processor in a lawyer's office. _____

4. You are working as a lifeguard at a public swimming pool.

   _____

5. You are serving food in a cafeteria. _____

B. Choose a partner. Think of other possible jobs. List these jobs and the clothes that would be right for each one.

Job: _____

Clothes: _____

Job: _____

Clothes: _____

LESSON REVIEW

Key Words and Ideas

Draw a line from the word to its correct definition.

1. dress code

2. casual clothes

3. pride

a) clothes worn when relaxing

b) feeling that you have importance

c) rules for what to wear in a certain place

Write the answers to the following questions on the lines.

4. What is one reason that it is important to dress correctly for work?

_____

5. How can you find out what clothes to wear for a new job?

_____

_____

Thinking About Dressing for Work

Circle the letter of the correct answer.

6. Which of the following is important to do?

   a) wear symbols on your clothing

   b) wear clothes that make it hard to work

   c) wear comfortable shoes

7. Good workers should

   a) wear whatever they feel like.

   b) wear a uniform if the job requires one.

   c) always wear casual clothes.

Workplace Workshop

8. Form a team with several other students. On a separate piece of paper, make a list of special clothing needs for the following jobs: nurse in a hospital, auto mechanic, cook, and airport baggage handler. Choose one of the jobs and create a dress code for new workers. Get the necessary information from interviewing people or looking at magazines.

It's Not Always Easy

Sometimes it's not easy to find the time to dress right for work. It's a good idea to get your clothes ready the night before. Why would it be helpful to choose your clothes then?

LESSON 11
GETTING TO WORK ON TIME

This lesson will help you answer this question:

- **How can you make sure to be on time for work?**

Words to Know:

schedule	a list of times to do things, a list of when things happen
reliable	able to be counted on and trusted
prompt	on time

Being on Time

The Hotel Statler, like all businesses, has a **schedule**. A schedule is a list of times to do things. According to the hotel's schedule, Ashley is supposed to be at work at 8:00 A.M. Ashley knows it is important to be on time. She is **reliable**. She knows that the hotel counts on her to do her job. If she is late, there will be problems. Other people will have to do her work, or the work won't get done.

When you work with other people, they count on you. They expect you to do your job. When workers are **prompt**, or on time, things can run smoothly. When they are late, the company's business cannot run well.

Here are some tips to help you be on time for work:

— Know how long it takes you to get ready for work. How long do you need to shower, to dress, to eat?

— Know how long it takes you to get to work. Do you have to worry about traffic or public transportation?

— Know how long it takes you to start work once you arrive. Do you have to change your clothes? Is there anything else you need to do before you start working?

— Before your first day of work, travel there to see how long it takes you.

How can you make sure to be on time for work?

Think about your answer to this question. Write your answer on a separate piece of paper. Discuss your ideas with a partner. Then make a list of these ideas.

WORKPLACE PRACTICE

This activity will give you practice at being on time.

A. Work with a partner to figure out how much time each of you needs for the following activities:

1. getting out of bed _____

2. taking a shower _____

3. getting dressed _____

4. eating breakfast _____

5. traveling to school _____

B. Write the total time it takes you to get ready in the morning.

_____

LESSON REVIEW

Key Words

Draw a line from the word to its correct definition.

1. schedule   a) a list of times to do things

2. prompt   b) on time

3. reliable   c) able to be counted on and trusted

Thinking About Getting to Work on Time

Circle the sentence that is true.

4. It doesn't matter if people come to work on time.

5. If Ashley is late, other people do her work.

Workplace Workshop

6. Ashley and a friend are listening to the weather report. They hear that the weather will be very bad. They both have to drive to work at rush hour on busy roads. Work with a classmate to show what they might say to each other to be sure they will get to work on time.

JOB TIP

Check your alarm clock to make sure it is working. It's a good habit to check it every night before you go to bed.

LESSON 12
UNDERSTANDING THE "BIG PICTURE"

Lesson Objective

This lesson will help you answer this question:

- **Why is it important to understand the "big picture"?**

Words to Know:

coworkers people you work with
contribute to play an important part

What Is the "Big Picture"?

The main goal of a company is called its "big picture." Providing good service to hotel guests is the "big picture" at the Hotel Statler.

Ashley and her **coworkers** work hard to meet the hotel's goals. Coworkers are the people you work with. Each employee has a job to do. People are needed to run the elevators, fix the lights, carry the luggage, and order the food. Ashley's role is to make sure the rooms are clean and that they have what they need. She fits into the hotel's "big picture" when she does a good job. She understands how her role contributes to the hotel's success. To **contribute** is to play an important part.

Understanding the "Big Picture"

Keep the following in mind as you think about how your job fits into the "big picture."

> — When you know how you fit into the "big picture," you feel important to the company.
>
> — When you know the main goals of a company, you can see how everyone is part of its success.
>
> — Knowing the goals of a company will help you understand the jobs of your coworkers.

Checkpoint

Why is it important to understand the "big picture"?

Think about your answer to this question. Write your answer on a separate piece of paper. Discuss your ideas with a partner. Then share these ideas with the class.

WORKPLACE PRACTICE

This activity will help you understand how you fit into the "big picture" of a company.

Suppose you work at a store that sells music CDs. Your job is to stock the shelves. Work with a partner to answer the following questions.

1. What is the "big picture" of the store?

   _____

2. How does your job fit into the "big picture"?

   _____

3. What would happen if you didn't stock the shelves?

   _____

LESSON REVIEW

Key Words

Circle the letter of the best definition of the words below.

1. coworkers

   a) customers   b) people you work with   c) goals

2. contribute

   a) to clean   b) to play an important part   c) to travel

Thinking About Understanding the "Big Picture"

Circle the letter of the correct answer.

3. A good worker should

   a) just learn his or her own job.   c) never ask questions.

   b) understand the whole company.

Workplace Workshop

4. Work in small groups to choose a company you would like to work for and a job you would like to do. Then write down the main goal of the company and how your job would be part of the "big picture." Share your ideas with other groups. Talk about the things you need to know about the company.

It's Not Always Easy

It may be hard to understand why some tasks are important. If you know the company's "big picture," these tasks may make more sense. Why are all tasks part of the "big picture"?

LESSON 13
FOLLOWING INSTRUCTIONS

Lesson Objective

This lesson will help you answer this question:

- **How can you make sure to follow instructions correctly?**

Words to Know:

instructions   orders about how to do something
vital   very important

Why—and How—to Follow Instructions

In the workplace, people will ask you to do many things. It is important to follow **instructions**, or orders, to get the job done correctly. In order to follow instructions correctly, you need to understand what you are supposed to do. Here are some tips for following instructions:

LISTEN CAREFULLY
To make sure she does the best job possible, Ashley listens carefully when her boss is talking to her. She pays close attention in order to remember all the details.

WRITE IT DOWN
Write down the *vital*—very important—information. Here are some things to do:

- If there are many parts to the instructions, make sure you understand each part.

- Number the order in which you will do each task.

- Be sure to write important names, dates, numbers, sizes, and other information correctly.

REPEAT THE INSTRUCTIONS
When someone gives you instructions, repeat them. Make sure you understand the task properly.

ASK QUESTIONS
If you are not sure about what to do, ask.

Checkpoint

How can you make sure you follow instructions correctly?

Think about your answer to this question. Write your answer on a separate piece of paper. Discuss your ideas with a partner. Then write these ideas in your journal or notebook.

WORKPLACE PRACTICE

This activity will give you practice at following instructions.

A. Read these instructions to a partner. Then have your partner repeat them to make sure he or she heard correctly.

You need to fix the following things in the hotel: two lamps and an air conditioner. Fix the air conditioner first.

B. Now have your partner read these instructions aloud. You repeat them in your own words.

First, clean the rooms on the second floor. Then clean the rooms on the tenth and eleventh floors. Make sure all the bathrooms have soap and fresh towels.

LESSON REVIEW

Key Words

Complete each sentence with a word from the box.

| instructions   vital |

JOB TIP

Remember that asking someone to repeat instructions is better than following them incorrectly.

1. Ashley remembers the _____ information because she writes it down.

2. Ashley's boss gives her important _____ for the day's work every morning.

Thinking About Following Instructions

Circle the sentence that is true.

3. You can think about other things and still easily remember what someone says to you.

4. If you write down what someone asks you to do, you will be sure to remember it.

Workplace Workshop

5. Ashley's boss, Mr. Johnson, is telling her about some special things that are needed in Room 112 of the hotel. With a partner, play the parts of Ashley and Mr. Johnson. Have Ashley show how she will remember all the items that are needed in the room.

LESSON 14
MANAGING TIME

This lesson will help you answer these questions:

- **Why is it important to know how much time you need?**
- **How can you plan your workday?**

Words to Know:

task	work that needs to be done
deadline	the date or time a task must be completed

Knowing the Time You Need

In school you have a fixed schedule. You are told where and when to go to certain classes. When you are working at a job, you usually have a whole day to finish one or more **tasks**. Some tasks, or work, take more time than others. It is usually up to you to figure out how to use your time. Your goal is to get the job done and meet your **deadline**. A deadline is the time a task must be completed.

Ashley knows that it usually takes her 25 minutes to clean a regular guest room. It takes her longer to clean larger rooms. Whatever job you do, keep track of how long it takes to complete. The next time you do it, you will know how much time you will need.

Ashley needs to know how much time it takes to clean a room.

Also, think about your own habits. You may need more time to do certain things than you need for others. To get the whole job done, you need to know how long each part of the job will take. You may want to keep this in mind as you plan your time.

Checkpoint

Why is it important to know how much time you will need?

Think about your answer to this question. Write your answer on a separate piece of paper. Discuss your ideas with a partner. Then illustrate these ideas in a poster. Display the poster in your classroom.

What Needs to Be Done?

Rob also works at the Hotel Statler. His job is to make sure that everything is in working order. He finds that a good way to manage his time is to make a "to do" list. Here's part of a "to do" list that Rob made one morning before he started to work:

TASK	ORDER OF TASK	SUPPLIES	TIME
fix bathtub - room 59	2	bring tools	30 min.
replace lightbulbs - room 102	4	bring extra lightbulbs	20 min.
fix curtain - room 98	3	may need new rod or cord	30 min.
replace broken chair - room 101	5	new chair	20 min.
fix air conditioner - room 12	1	tool box	1 hour

Here are some things to do to help you manage your time:

- Make a "to do" list. Write down every task or meeting you have.
- Number each task according to how important it is. Think about what you were hired to do. Which task is most important to your job?
- Figure out how long each task will take to complete.
- Write down the supplies you'll need for the job.
- Think about what your work habits are like.
- Set up a schedule showing when you will do each job.

It's Not Always Easy

It's not always easy to figure out how much time a task will take. You might want to ask your boss or a coworker what he or she expects. Why is it important to know how long a task should take?

How can you plan your workday?

Think about your answer to this question. Write your answer on a separate piece of paper. Discuss your ideas with a partner. Then write any new ideas in a paragraph.

Checkpoint

This activity will help you practice managing your time.

A. Suppose you are planning what to do today at work. First, choose one of the jobs from the list below. Then make a "to do" list of all the tasks you think you would have to do during one day. Number each task according to its importance. For each task, write the supplies you think you'll need. Then write the amount of time you think it will take.

bicycle messenger in a large city

salesperson in a video store

car mechanic

chef in a restaurant

plumber

secretary in an office

Task	Order of Task	Supplies	Time

B. Choose a partner. Look at one another's lists. Offer suggestions to each other. Change or add to your list where necessary.

C. Share your lists with the class.

LESSON REVIEW

Key Words and Ideas

Write the word below that answers the question.

task	deadline

1. What describes the latest time when something must be done?

   _____

2. What is another word for work that needs to be done?

   _____

Write the answer to the following question on the line.

3. Why is it important to know how much time it takes you to do a job?

   _____

Thinking About Managing Time

Circle the letter of the correct answer.

4. Which of the following is a good way to manage time?

   a) do the least important task first

   b) make a list of things to do at the beginning of each day

   c) think that every job takes the same amount of time

5. People who are good at managing time will

   a) plan their vacation while at work.

   b) spend a lot of time talking to coworkers about cars.

   c) think about how long each job will take.

Workplace Workshop

6. Work with a small group to prepare a brief talk to a class of younger students. The talk will be about how to manage time in order to meet deadlines. Be sure to include why it is important for the students to plan their day by figuring out what needs to be done and how long each task will take.

JOB TIP

Keep a date book to write down what you need to do each day. Look at the date book the night before to help plan the next day.

LESSON 15
BEING ORGANIZED

This lesson will help you answer these questions:

- **Why should you organize your work?**
- **What are good ways to be organized in the workplace?**

Words to Know:

organize	arrange in a certain order
records	information that is saved
receipt	a slip of paper that shows how much money was paid for something

Reasons to Be Organized

Ashley knows that her job goes well when she is organized. To **organize** things, she arranges her materials in a certain order. She places the towels in the same spot on her cart each day. She does the same with the tissues, soap, and other things that go in the rooms. The products she uses to clean are also in order. Ashley knows that if she keeps her cart neat, she can find everything quickly.

Being organized saves Ashley time.

No matter where you work, there are many good reasons to be organized. You can save a lot of time when you are able to find a memo or tool when you want it. Also, if someone asks you for an item, you can find it right away. Stopping to look for something can waste time. Work goes much more smoothly when you can find things quickly.

Why should you organize your work?

Think about your answer to this question. Write your answer on a separate piece of paper. Discuss your ideas with a partner. Then share your ideas with the class.

What Should Be Kept?

Records are pieces of information that are important enough to save. Records that people keep include copies of memos or letters that are sent or received. People also like to keep receipts. A **receipt** is a slip of paper that shows how much money was paid for an item.

How to Organize Information

It's important to organize information in a way that is useful. Your record-keeping system will be useful if you can find things when you need them. Here are a few ways to organize information:

— FOLDERS:
It's a good idea to keep papers in file folders. On the tab of each folder, write the kind of record—for instance, *Memos, Bills, Receipts.* You can keep folders in file cabinets, in alphabetical order.

— COMPUTERS:
Many companies store information on computers. You will learn more about computers in Lesson 32.

— CASH REGISTERS:
When you work in a store, you will usually keep money in a cash register. The different bills and coins are kept in separate parts of the cash register drawer.

— CHARTS:
Charts are useful for recording information that people can easily see. For instance, charts are hung up on hospital walls. The hospital workers' schedules are written down on the charts.

It's Not Always Easy

At times, you may be too busy to organize your things. But, it is good to get in the habit of filing things right away. The neater your filing system is, the easier you will be able to find things later. What are some records that you can file?

What are good ways to be organized in the workplace?

Think about your answer to this question. Write your answer on a separate piece of paper. Discuss your ideas with a partner. Then share these ideas with the class.

Checkpoint

This activity will help you practice being organized.

Suppose you are an assistant to the manager of a store that sells sports equipment. You deal with several kinds of information.

A. Here are some of the items. Read about them and answer the questions on the lines.

1. You have received letters from customers. Some of the letters tell you how happy people are with your company's products. Some of the letters tell you how you should improve the products. You want to keep both types of letters. How would you organize these letters?

   _____

2. Your boss asks you to keep track of the schedules of the other company employees. What is a good way to organize this information so that everyone can see what the schedules are?

   _____

3. You have just waited on five customers. They have paid you for the items they bought. You have 18 one-dollar bills, 5 ten-dollar bills, 3 five-dollar bills, and 4 checks. How will you organize these payments?

   _____

4. Employee information is kept in folders. Each employee has a folder that has letters of reference, a résumé, vacation schedules, and employment history. Your boss hands you the stack of folders. Where would you put the folders?

   _____

5. There is a pile of receipts from the customers' purchases. You know these are important to keep. Where will you put them?

   _____

B. Choose a partner.

6. Discuss with your partner the ways in which you have organized the information. Make changes to your answers if necessary.

LESSON REVIEW

Key Words and Ideas

Write the word next to the correct definition below.

record	receipt	organize

1. information that is saved _____

2. arrange in a certain way _____

3. a slip of paper that shows how much money was spent

   _____

Write the answers to the following questions on the lines.

4. Why is it a good idea to be organized in the workplace?

   _____

5. What are two good ways to manage information?

   _____

   _____

Thinking About Being Organized

Circle the letter of the correct answer.

6. Which of the following is a reason to be neat at work?

   a) It makes things much harder to find.

   b) It can save you time when you need to find something.

   c) You can never prove if you paid for something with a check.

7. Where would be the best place to keep receipts if you ran a store?

   a) in a computer   c) in a folder in a filing cabinet

   b) in the cash register

Workplace Workshop

8. Work in groups of three or four. Choose a store in your community. Then work individually to list the kinds of records the store manager would need to keep. When you have created lists, work together to make a group list. Then decide the best way to store each item. Share your ideas with other groups. Work as a class to list the most common needs and forms of record keeping.

LESSON 16
BEING RESPONSIBLE

Lesson Objectives

This lesson will help you answer these questions:

- **Why do employers need to count on their workers?**
- **How can you be a responsible worker?**

Words to Know:

responsible doing what you are supposed to do
priority a level of importance

What It Means to Be Responsible

Ashley knows what it means to be **responsible** at work. She shows up on time and does the best job she can. She understands how important it is to be responsible and to be trusted by her coworkers. They can count on Ashley to do her share of the work.

Ashley's coworkers know they can count on her.

A job is an exchange. An employer gives you a salary in exchange for the work you do. The company is responsible for paying you and you are responsible for doing the job you were hired to do.

Your employers are running a business. They count on you and the other workers to carry out the business of the company. They cannot have success without responsible workers.

They want to see that doing a good job is a **priority** for you. They want to know that it is important to you. A worker who is not responsible can easily lose a job. A responsible worker is one that an employer wants to keep for many years.

Checkpoint

Why do employers need to count on their workers?

Think about your answer to this question. Write your answer on a separate piece of paper. Discuss your ideas with a partner. Then combine your ideas on a list and read it to the class.

How to Become a Responsible Worker

There are many ways that you can be a responsible worker. Just remember how much other people are counting on you. Here are some tips for being responsible that Ashley jotted down:

TIPS FOR BEING RESPONSIBLE

✔ **Always come to work on time.**

✔ **Follow all instructions.**

✔ **Don't say that you can do something that you know you can't do.**

✔ **Do the best job that you can.**

✔ **Be polite to everyone.**

JOB TIP

A responsible worker will tell a boss when it is not possible to do a job. The boss can then get more help or find another way to get the job done.

When You Can't Get to Work

Once in a while there is a good reason to miss work. If you're sick, it may not be possible for you to get to your job. Responsible workers let people at work know that they will not be able to do their job that day.

When you cannot get to work, you must make sure that you call your boss as soon as you can. Your boss needs to be able to plan the workday without you. There may be a need to have someone else do your job for that day. If you are sick for more than a few days, you may have to ask your doctor to write a note explaining your illness.

How can you be a responsible worker?

Think about your answer to this question. Write your answer on a separate piece of paper. Discuss your ideas with a partner. Then share any new ideas with your class.

Checkpoint

This activity will help you think about what it takes to be a responsible worker.

A. Read each situation below and then answer the questions.

1. You work as a carpenter's assistant five days a week. On Tuesday evening you cut your finger badly and need to get three stitches. The doctor says that you should not work for two days. What should you do?

   _____

   _____

   _____

2. Pam works at a restaurant as a waitress. She is late to work almost every day. What do you think her employer should tell her? What steps can she take to get to work on time?

   _____

   _____

   _____

3. On Wednesday, your boss asks you if you'd be willing to work an extra day on Saturday. You agree to come to work. On Friday, your best friend invites you to go to the beach the next day. Should you go to work or to the beach on Saturday? Why?

   _____

   _____

   _____

4. Ginger is a salesclerk at a large clothing store. Each day she helps customers buy clothes. She enters each sale on the computer and takes the payments. What are three ways that her employers count on her? In what ways do the customers count on her?

   _____

   _____

   _____

B. Choose a partner. Discuss your answers with your partner.

LESSON REVIEW

Key Words and Ideas

Write the word next to the correct definition.

responsible	priority

1. a level of importance _____

2. doing what you are supposed to do _____

Write the answer to the following question on the lines.

3. Why should people be able to count on you at work?

_____

_____

Thinking About Being Responsible

Circle the letter of the correct answer.

4. Which of the following is a reason to be absent from work?

   a) being too tired to get up in the morning

   b) getting the flu

   c) a good baseball game

   d) a chance to go to the beach

5. How can you avoid being late for work?

   a) Don't pay attention to your clothing.

   b) Call and let your boss know you are going to be late.

   c) Stay up late at night.

   d) Know how long it usually takes to get ready and then allow extra time.

Workplace Workshop

6. Work in groups of five. Suppose that you work together at a restaurant. You can take the roles of cook, server, dishwasher, host or hostess, and customer. Show the class how you work together when a customer enters the restaurant. Tell why your coworkers count on you. When each group has finished, discuss what you have learned about the importance of being a responsible worker.

Unit 3 Review
Being a Good Worker

In this unit you learned about:

- Dressing for Work
- Getting to Work on Time
- Understanding the "Big Picture"
- Following Instructions
- Managing Time
- Being Organized
- Being Responsible

I. Vocabulary

Write the letter of the correct definition next to each word.

____ 1. casual clothes

____ 2. dress code

____ 3. schedule

____ 4. prompt

____ 5. reliable

____ 6. contribute

____ 7. vital

____ 8. deadline

____ 9. task

a) on time

b) rules for what to wear in a certain place, such as a job or restaurant

c) to play an important part

d) a list of times to do things, a list of when things happen

e) clothes worn when relaxing, such as around the home, at a picnic, or while playing

f) very important

g) the date or time a task must be completed

h) work that needs to be done

i) able to de counted on and trusted

Fill in the blank in each sentence with a word from the box.

records	pride	organize	priority
instructions	responsible	receipt	coworkers

10. Ashley's boss knows she is a _____ worker because she is always on time.

11. She knows she does a good job, and takes _____ in her work.

12. James listened carefully to the _____ on how to do the job.

13. Sarah likes to _____ her shelves by putting important things up front.

14. When Gina bought the scarf, she got a _____ that showed how much she paid for it.

15. Because neatness was a _____ for Sam, he cleaned up his work station.

16. Kevin wanted the _____ that showed the information on last year's sales.

17. Jake and his _____ played on the company's baseball team.

II. Main Ideas

Circle the letter of the correct answer.

18. It is important to dress correctly and be on time for work because

   a) you might meet a friend or relative.

   b) you want to make a good impression on your boss, other workers, and clients.

   c) someone might ask you out to lunch.

19. You can be sure to remember instructions by

   a) listening carefully and taking notes.

   b) listening to the radio while someone is speaking to you.

   c) thinking about what you are going to do after work.

III. What Would You Do?

Write your answers to the questions on the lines.

20. You have a new job as a cashier in a clothing store. You want to choose the best clothes to wear to work. What is one question you will ask yourself?

   _____

21. You just got a job as a receptionist for a large company. Why is it a good idea to find out what the "big picture" is?

   _____

22. Your boss calls you into her office on Monday and tells you six things that she wants done by the end of the week. How will you remember to do them all?

   _____

23. Your boss asks you to close up the shop. You're not sure what you are supposed to do with the keys. What should you do?

_____

IV. Solving Workplace Problems

24. Jennifer is in charge of her company's mail room. Henry, one of her employees, is late to work one or two days a week. What should Jennifer say to him in order to change the situation?

_____

_____

25. What are two reasons for an employee to be on time for work?

_____

_____

V. Unit Replay

Go back to the story on page 41. Reread it. Ask yourself again: What do you think it takes to be a good worker? Write your answer on a separate piece of paper.

VI. You . . . and Being A Good Worker

Check ✔ the boxes next to the questions you can answer now.
Write an ✗ next to the ones you think you need to work on more.

❑ Why is it important to dress correctly for work? (Lesson 10)

❑ How can you be sure to wear the right clothes? (Lesson 10)

❑ How can you make sure to be on time for work? (Lesson 11)

❑ Why is it important to understand "the big picture"? (Lesson 12)

❑ How can you make sure to follow instructions correctly? (Lesson 13)

❑ Why is it important to know how much time you need? (Lesson 14)

❑ How can you plan your workday? (Lesson 14)

❑ Why should you organize your work? (Lesson 15)

❑ What are good ways to be organized in the workplace? (Lesson 15)

❑ Why do employers need to count on their workers? (Lesson 16)

❑ How can you be a responsible worker? (Lesson 16)

If you put an ✗ next to any question, go back and review the lesson.

Unit 4
Communicating at Work

A BUSY DAY AT PETE'S DRY CLEANERS

Manuel worked at Pete's Dry Cleaners. The phone rang all the time. On Thursday morning, Mrs. Hernandez called to ask: "Are my clothes ready to be picked up?"

A few minutes later, Jim Lu called with a question: "Can you take paint out of a woolen rug?"

There were also customers to take care of in the store.

Phil Russo stopped in to complain. He pointed to his jacket and said, "The coffee stain is still there!"

Marie Cooper wanted to see the tailor. He wasn't in. Marie asked Manuel: "Would you give him a message? I'd like him to fix a skirt zipper. Can he call me to make an appointment? Thanks."

Manuel dealt with many people every day. He had to be careful how he treated each one of them.

What Do You Think?

How would you treat the various kinds of people at work? How can different people understand each other?

Communicating with different people is an important part of the job. In this unit, you will learn about:

- Understanding One Another
- Using the Telephone
- Being Polite
- Asking for Help
- Treating Customers
- Handling Criticism
- Offering an Apology

LESSON 17
UNDERSTANDING ONE ANOTHER

Lesson Objectives

This lesson will help you to answer these questions:

- **Why do people need to understand one another at work?**
- **How can you communicate well in the workplace?**

Words to Know:

communicate	to share thoughts, feelings, and ideas with others
body language	showing feelings using your body and your face

The Importance of Understanding

A business runs well when everyone—employees, customers, employers, coworkers—can **communicate**. They communicate when they can share thoughts, feelings, and ideas with each other. People mostly communicate by talking to one another. They also communicate with **body language**, or using their body or face to show what they mean.

Manuel understands what his customers need.

When Manuel and his customers understand each other:

- he knows what kind of service his customers need.
- he can let his customers know what he will do for them.

When Manuel and his boss, Pete, understand each other:

- he knows what Pete wants him to do.
- he can let Pete know what he needs.

Why do people need to understand one another at work?

Think about your answer to this question. Write your answer on a separate piece of paper. Discuss your ideas with a partner. Then present your ideas to the class.

Checkpoint

Be a Good Communicator

Good communication is necessary for the workplace. People need to express what they want from one another to get the job done. Whether you're working in an office, a store, a restaurant, an airport, or a factory, good communication skills will help you at your job.

To communicate in the workplace, here are some tips:

> Greet customers with a smile and ask, *"May I help you?"*
>
> Tell people you enjoy having their business.
>
> Pay attention when others express themselves.
>
> Stand up straight, look people in the eye, and speak clearly.
>
> Watch your body language. Don't slouch or sigh.
>
> Be careful not to interrupt when someone is speaking.
>
> Remember to say *"please"* and *"thank you."*
>
> Think before you speak. Figure out what you mean to say before you say it.
>
> Get to the point. Try not to waste people's time at work.

It's Not Always Easy

It's hard to feel angry and not be able to show it openly. But the workplace is not the right place to get angry. Why is anger bad for the workplace?

Sometimes a person will make you angry. If anger is communicated in the wrong way, it can disturb the workplace.

Here are some tips if you get angry:

- Wait for a good time to express yourself. Make sure the other person has the time to listen.

- Focus on how bad you feel about the situation, not on how bad the other person is. If you want to communicate your feelings, say "I am hurt that you did that." Do not say "You are a terrible person because you did that."

- Be careful not to shout or yell.

- Choose your words carefully to explain how you would like things to change.

- Listen carefully when the other person explains.

- If you accept the explanation, let the person know that you understand.

How can you communicate well in the workplace?

Think about your answer to this question. Write your answer on a separate piece of paper. Discuss your ideas with a partner. Then share these ideas with your class.

Checkpoint

WORKPLACE PRACTICE

This activity will help you to practice communicating with others.

Suppose you work in a shoe store. Mrs. O'Brien comes in with a box of shoes that she bought and wore to a party. She wants to return them because they hurt her feet. You know that the store has a policy to not take used shoes back.

A. Answer the following questions on the lines.

1. What do you say to Mrs. O'Brien when she walks into the store?

   _____

   _____

   _____

2. What do you say to Mrs. O'Brien when she says she wants to return the shoes?

   _____

   _____

   _____

3. You turn away for a moment. Tiffany, a coworker, walks in and starts to wait on Mrs. O'Brien. This makes you angry. What do you say to Tiffany?

   _____

   _____

   _____

4. Tiffany explains that she didn't realize Mrs. O'Brien was your customer. What do you say to Tiffany?

   _____

   _____

   _____

B. Choose a partner and role-play the following activity.

5. Ned, a worker in the shoe store, has a doctor's appointment. He wants to ask the boss for permission to leave early. What does Ned say to his boss? How does his boss respond? Take turns with your partner playing the roles of Ned and the boss.

JOB TIP

When you want to communicate to a coworker that you are unhappy about something, do it privately. No one else has to hear it.

LESSON REVIEW

Key Words and Ideas

Draw a line from the word to its definition.

1. communicate

a) to share thoughts, feelings, and ideas with others

2. body language

b) showing feelings using your body and your face

Write your answers to the following questions on the lines.

3. Why is it important to communicate well in the workplace? List two reasons in your answer.

_____

_____

4. What are two ways to communicate well at work?

_____

_____

Thinking About Understanding One Another

Circle the letter of the correct answer.

5. How can you make sure that people understand you?

a) talk for a long time

b) look the other way

c) think before you speak

6. People can understand each other if they

a) listen to each other.

b) argue.

c) interrupt each other.

Workplace Workshop

7. Pete is hiring two more workers. He wants Manuel to teach them communication skills. With a partner, play the roles of Manuel and a customer. Have a conversation that shows the new workers how to communicate well. Then exchange roles.

LESSON 18
USING THE TELEPHONE

This lesson will help you answer the following questions:

- **How can telephones be used in the workplace?**
- **How can you be helpful on the telephone?**

Words to Know:

answering machine	a machine that records telephone messages
fax machine	a machine that sends and receives information on paper using a phone line

Know What Phones Can Do

Many people call Pete's Dry Cleaners. Manuel takes different kinds of messages. Some customers want to know if their clothing is ready to be picked up. Some want to set up a time for the tailor to fix something. There are times when Manuel has to transfer calls to other employees in the store.

When Manuel takes a message, he is careful to take down all the information.

Attached to the phone is an **answering machine.** It records messages when the shop is closed. When Manuel gets to work, he listens to the recorded messages. Then he writes down the names of the callers, their phone numbers, and the messages that they've left.

Sometimes people send messages through the **fax machine.** This is a machine that uses the phone line to send and receive messages on paper. Manuel puts these in a neat pile for Pete to read when he gets in.

How can telephones be used in the workplace?

Think about your answer to this question. Write your answer on a separate piece of paper. Discuss your ideas with a partner. Then list your ideas and share them with your class.

Checkpoint

Using the Phone

"Hello, Pete's Dry Cleaners. This is Manuel. How can I help you?"

Manuel has a lot of experience talking on the phone. He is proud of the way he communicates with customers on the phone. Read Manuel's tips for using the phone and taking messages in the workplace.

When Using the Phone

- answer quickly
- speak clearly
- make sure your voice sounds pleasant
- ask politely who is calling
- ask how you can help
- transfer calls carefully
- ask people if they would like to leave a message before putting them on hold

When Taking a Message

- write the caller's complete name.
- write the caller's company, telephone number, and the time and date of the call
- write the message neatly

When Leaving a Message

- give your name
- explain why you are calling
- speak slowly and clearly
- leave your phone number and the time you called

It's Not Always Easy

It's sometimes hard to understand what someone is saying on the phone. It's okay to say, "I'm sorry. I didn't hear what you said. Can you repeat that information?" Why is it important to make sure you hear information correctly?

How can you be helpful on the telephone?

Think about your answer to this question. Write your answer on a separate piece of paper. Discuss your ideas with a partner. Then write your ideas on an index card.

Checkpoint

WORKPLACE PRACTICE

This activity will help you practice taking telephone messages.

JOB TIP

Repeat the caller's name and phone number to be sure your message is correct.

Suppose that you and a partner work at Pete's Dry Cleaners. Two customers call and leave messages.

Choose a partner. For Message #1, play the part of the customer and have your partner write down the message. Exchange roles for Message #2.

Message #1: Call made on Nov. 17, 1999 at 11 A.M.

"Hello, this is Mrs. Barker. I'd like to have two pairs of pants shortened. When will the tailor be able to see me? I am free any morning this week. Please call and let me know. My number is 555-5567."

Telephone Message

Date_____ Time _____
Name of caller _____
Message _____
_____
_____
Message taken by _____

Message #2: Call made on Nov. 17, 1999 at 3:30 P.M.

"This is Kim Daley. I dropped off a suit and a dress to be cleaned. When will they be ready? I'd love to pick them up today if possible. Call me at work. My number is 555-7583. Thanks."

Telephone Message

Date_____ Time _____
Name of caller _____
Message _____
_____
_____
Message taken by _____

LESSON REVIEW

Key Words and Ideas

Draw a line from the word to its correct definition.

1. a fax machine

    a) a machine that sends and receives information on paper using a phone line

2. answering machine

    b) a machine that records messages

Write the answer to the following questions on the lines.

3. Why is it important to write down a message correctly?

_____

4. What are three rules for answering the phone?

_____

_____

_____

Thinking About Using the Telephone

Circle the letter of the correct answer.

5. When taking a telephone message, you should
    a) write quickly and hang up.
    b) write the caller's full name.
    c) write only the caller's first name.

6. What could happen if telephone messages were not taken correctly?
    a) customers would be happy
    b) important information could be missed
    c) the telephone would stop ringing

Workplace Workshop

7. Suppose you are a receptionist and take all the messages for your company. It is Monday morning. There are messages on the answering machine. There are faxes in the fax machine. The phone rings, and it is for your boss. Discuss with a partner the things you need to do.

LESSON 19
BEING POLITE

Lesson Objective

This lesson will help you answer this question:

- **How can you be polite in the workplace?**

Words to Know:

considerate   thoughtful and caring about others
atmosphere   the mood of a place

Politeness Is Good for Business

People like to be treated well. Manuel tries hard to be **considerate**. He uses kind and polite words. He says, "please" and "thank you." He tries to remember his customers' names. He chooses his words carefully and tries to say the right thing. This makes people feel good. They will tell others about his store, and they will come back.

In the workplace, it is also important for employees to be polite with each other. When everyone is polite to one another, the **atmosphere**—the mood of the place—is pleasant. People will want to work there, and customers will want to come to do business.

Good manners makes everyone feel good. Read the following tips about how to be polite.

- Always say "*please*" when you are asking someone to do something.
- Say "*thank you*" when someone has given you something or done something for you.
- Do not interrupt when someone is speaking.
- If you bump into someone by mistake, say "*excuse me.*"
- Hold the door for a person who is behind you.
- Be patient with people who may need a little extra time to do something.

Checkpoint

How can you be polite in the workplace?

Think about your answer to this question. Write your answer on a separate piece of paper. Discuss your ideas with a partner. Then present your ideas to the class.

WORKPLACE PRACTICE

This activity will give you practice being polite.

Suppose you work in a stationery store. You are about to close the store when Mrs. Brown arrives. You are worried about being late to meet your friend, but you let Mrs. Brown in. How do you treat her? Think about how you can let her know you would like to close the store.

Work with a partner to answer the following questions.

1. What will you say that will be polite to Mrs. Brown?

   _____

   _____

2. What should Mrs. Brown say to you?

   _____

   _____

LESSON REVIEW

Key Words

Complete each sentence with a word from the box.

> considerate   atmosphere

1. The _____ in the office was pleasant.

2. It is good manners to be _____ of people's feelings.

Thinking About Being Polite

Write the answer to the following question on the line.

3. Why is it important to be polite in the workplace?

   _____

Workplace Workshop

4. You are waiting on a customer in a shoe store. Another customer breaks in to ask you a question. Role-play with two classmates the parts of the salesperson and the customers.

JOB TIP

If you are in a bad mood, do your best not to show it at work. Feeling bad is not an excuse for being rude on the job.

LESSON 20
ASKING FOR HELP

This lesson will help you answer this question:

- **How can you ask for help when you need it?**

Words to Know:

assist to give help
tone a way of speaking that shows a certain feeling

When to Ask for Help

When Manuel doesn't know something, he asks questions. He has seen that if you try to do something without knowing how, you make mistakes. Pete is happy to answer questions. Manuel's questions show that he wants to do things the right way.

In the workplace, it is important to ask for help when you need it. Let a coworker or your boss know you have a question, and figure out the best time to ask it. Remember, if you have a question and don't ask it, you will make mistakes. That may cost the company time and money.

How to Ask

There are things to think about when you ask someone for help. The following tips will be useful when you need someone to **assist** you.

- Always be polite and use a friendly *tone* of voice. If you are nasty, no one will want to help you.

- Don't demand that someone help you. People should want to help you. They should not feel as if they have to.

- Make sure the person has time. If it is not a good time, ask when you should come back.

- When you ask a question, you may not understand everything the first time. Don't be afraid to ask again.

How can you ask for help when you need it?

Think about your answer to this question. Write your answer on a separate piece of paper. Discuss your ideas with a partner. Then write your ideas on a note card, and share them with the class.

WORKPLACE PRACTICE

This activity will give you practice in asking for help.

You have a new job at Pete's Dry Cleaners. On your first day, the two situations below occur.

Choose a partner. Play the part of the worker and your partner can play the part of Pete. Then exchange roles.

1. One day you are alone at the counter. Pete is in his office. There are eight people in line. They are beginning to complain. How can you ask for help? What tone will you use?

2. Mrs. Hernandez wants to know if her skirt can be ready by Monday. You need to ask Pete. Pete is waiting on another customer. How do you ask Pete for help?

LESSON REVIEW

Key Words

Underline the word that best completes each sentence.

1. When I spoke to him on the phone, I noticed that he had a good (tone, coach).

2. When you are having a problem, you want someone to (assist, question) you.

JOB TIP

Never be afraid to say you don't understand something.

Thinking About Asking for Help

Circle the sentence that is true.

3. The best workers never ask for help.

4. Asking for help will save time and solve problems.

Workplace Workshop

5. Mr. Lopez asks Manuel if Pete can get the stain out of his shirt by tomorrow. Pete is not in the store. Manuel doesn't know the answer. What should he tell Mr. Lopez? Role-play the situation.

LESSON 21
TREATING CUSTOMERS

This lesson will help you answer these questions:

- **Why is it important to treat customers well?**
- **How can you be helpful to a customer?**

Words to Know:

clients   customers
attitude   a way of acting that shows what someone is feeling or thinking

When You Are a Customer

When you are a customer, you want attention. If you have a problem, you want it solved. When you enter a store, you want to feel welcome. You want to know that you will be treated well. When a salesperson gives you good service, you will want to go back to that store. Manuel and Pete know how to treat customers. They know how they like to be treated when they are customers.

Customers like the service they get at Pete's Dry Cleaners.

No Customers, No Business

A business depends on its **clients** or customers. People have a choice of places to go to do business. If customers aren't satisfied with the service they get, they go someplace else. Mrs. Jackson depends on getting good service at Pete's. She likes Manuel's helpful **attitude**. This attitude helps keep Pete's business going. Manuel and Pete treat every customer well. The customers then tell others to go to Pete's, too.

Why is it important to treat customers well?

Think about your answer to this question. Write your answer on a separate piece of paper. Talk over your ideas with a partner. Brainstorm some new ones and share them with the class.

Checkpoint

How to Be Helpful to Customers

Manuel has a good attitude. He approaches his customers pleasantly and helpfully. He knows that Pete cares about his customers. His job is to make the customer happy. Manuel found these rules for treating customers in a newspaper. Read them.

Be Helpful to Your Customers

What You Should Do . . .

- ask how you can help

- explain the services your business offers

- listen to clients' problems and suggestions

- have a helpful attitude

- treat all customers fairly

- remember clients' names

- never argue with a customer

- always remain calm

- never tell a customer that he or she is wrong

- always do your best so you will be proud of your work

If You Don't Know What to Do

- ask your supervisor for help

- ask your customers how you can serve them better

- suggest that your client talk with your boss

It's Not Always Easy

Some customers are not easy to deal with. But do your best to treat them with respect. How do you like to be treated when you are a customer?

How can you be helpful to customers?

Think about your answer to this question. Write your answer on a separate piece of paper. Discuss your ideas with a partner. Then make a list for the class.

Checkpoint

WORKPLACE PRACTICE

This activity will give you practice treating customers well.

Suppose that you work in John's hardware store. It is Saturday morning, and the store is very busy. John is in the back cutting window glass. Mr. Cho needs some glass cut. Mrs. Hardy wants help choosing paint for her living room. There are three people waiting in line to pay for their tools and supplies.

A. Write the answers to the following questions on the lines.

1. What can you say to the people waiting in line?

_____

_____

_____

2. How can you help Mr. Cho?

_____

_____

_____

3. What can you suggest to Mrs. Hardy?

_____

_____

_____

B. Choose a partner. Role-play the following situations.

4. One of the customers on line says that he can't wait any longer. What does the store clerk do?

5. Mrs. Hardy is a very good customer. She left her wallet at home and has no money to pay for the paint. How should she be treated?

JOB TIP

There may be times when you are very busy. Customers are waiting. Tell them you will take care of them as soon as you can. People will understand, as long as you show them some attention.

LESSON REVIEW

Key Words and Ideas

Draw a line from the word to its correct definition.

1. clients

2. attitude

a) a way of acting that shows what someone is feeling or thinking

b) customers

Write the answers to the following questions on the lines.

3. Why is it important to treat customers well?

_____

4. Why should you keep a good attitude?

_____

Thinking About Treating Customers

Circle the letter of the correct answer.

5. Which of the following would be a good way to treat customers?

   a) ask how you can help

   b) ignore them

   c) go on a break if you need one

   d) tell them to come back later

6. Which of the following is **not** a good reason to help clients?

   a) it is good for business

   b) you care about people

   c) you can be proud of giving good service

   d) they will give you gifts

Workplace Workshop

7. Mr. Gomez just walked into Pete's Dry Cleaners. He complains every time he comes in. Discuss the problem with a partner. Then write your ideas below. How should Manuel treat Mr. Gomez? What should he do and say? You and your partner act out their conversation.

LESSON 22
HANDLING CRITICISM

Lesson Objective

This lesson will help you answer this question:

- **How can people give and receive criticism?**

Words to Know:

feedback	information people give you about your work
criticize	to find fault with something
constructive criticism	tips that help someone improve

Giving Criticism

It is important for employees to know if their work is good or if it needs to improve. It is important for them to get **feedback**. Feedback from an employer helps an employee know how well he or she is doing.

Pete thinks it's important to help employees by giving them feedback. When he needs to **criticize** Manuel for doing something wrong, he is careful not to hurt Manuel's feelings. Pete uses a friendly tone. He begins by saying something nice. Then he gives Manuel **constructive criticism**. Constructive criticism gives Manuel tips that will help him improve.

Receiving Criticism

Constructive criticism is useful if you want to do the best job you can. Here are some tips about how to receive criticism.

- Listen closely. Remember, it is your work—not you—that is being criticized.
- Ask questions to make sure you understand the criticism.
- Make sure you understand how to correct whatever needs to be corrected.
- After correcting your work, ask if you are doing it the right way.

Checkpoint

How can people give and receive criticism?

Think about your answer to this question. Write your answer on a separate piece of paper. Discuss your ideas with a partner. Make a list of your ideas and read it to the class.

WORKPLACE PRACTICE

This activity will help you think about criticism.

Stacy, Manuel's coworker, has been late every day this week. Other workers are complaining. They can't go home until she arrives. Her boss, Pete, wants to give her some constructive criticism.

A. Answer the following questions.

What does Pete say to Stacy?

_____

How should Stacy respond to Pete?

_____

B. Choose a partner. Role-play the parts of Pete and Stacy.

LESSON REVIEW

Key Words

Write the correct word next to its definition.

constructive criticism   feedback   criticize

1. to find fault with something _____

2. information people give you about your work _____

3. tips that help someone improve _____

Thinking About Handling Criticism

Circle the sentence that is true.

4. Constructive criticism is supposed to make people feel bad.

5. Constructive criticism can help people improve their work.

Workplace Workshop

6. Henry spends too much time at the coffee machine. His boss, Ms. Sakura, is upset. What should Ms. Sakura say? How should Henry respond? With a partner, role-play a conversation between Ms. Sakura and Henry.

JOB TIP

If you have to criticize someone, be sure to say what you like as well as what you don't like.

LESSON 23
OFFERING AN APOLOGY

This lesson will help you to answer this question:

- **How should you make an apology?**

Words to Know:

apologize	saying you're sorry
regret	to be sorry for something

Why Make an Apology?

Mrs. Fox shows Manuel a stain that the cleaners didn't get out of a dress. Manuel says he is sorry. He says the dress will be cleaned again without charge. Mrs. Fox is happy that her problem is being handled well.

Sometimes in the workplace you have to say that you are sorry. Perhaps your company made a mistake. You are a part of the company. You may have to **apologize** for something it did wrong.

Sometimes coworkers say or do something that causes a problem. Then the person has to apologize. An apology shows people that you are sorry. It tells them that you **regret** what happened. It makes it possible for work to continue. Everyone feels better.

How to Make a Good Apology

Here are some things to think about when you make an apology.

- Be sure the time is right. If the person is very busy, try another time.

- Look at the person when you make your apology.

- Say you are sorry. Say that you'll try to make sure it doesn't happen again.

- Listen politely if the person has something else to tell you.

How should you make an apology?

Think about your answer to this question. Write your answer on a separate piece of paper. Discuss your ideas with a partner. Then explain your ideas to the class.

WORKPLACE PRACTICE

This activity will give you practice at making an apology.

Last Tuesday, Pete got a phone call when he was not in the store. Manuel wrote down the message. He forgot to write the caller's phone number. Pete was upset. Manuel knows he made a mistake.

Choose a partner. Discuss the following questions with your partner. Then write your ideas on the line.

1. Why should Manuel apologize?

   _____

2. What should Manuel say?

   _____

LESSON REVIEW

Key Words

Draw a line from the word to its correct definition.

1. regret
2. apologize

a) to be sorry about something you did
b) to say you're sorry

Thinking About Offering an Apology

Circle the letter of the correct answer.

3. When you make an apology that has worked,

   a) everyone feels worse.

   b) work stops.

   c) everyone knows that you are sorry.

Workplace Workshop

4. Terry took Kim's pen without asking. Kim didn't have it when she needed it. Kim is very angry. Terry said she was in a hurry. Work with a partner to resolve this problem. Should someone apologize? Why? What should both workers say? Role-play a conversation.

JOB TIP

Make an apology as soon as you can. If you wait too long, the apology will not seem important.

Unit 4 Review
Communicating at Work

In this unit you learned about:

- Understanding One Another
- Using the Telephone
- Being Polite
- Asking for Help

- Treating Customers
- Handling Criticism
- Offering an Apology

I. Vocabulary

Write the letter of the correct definition next to each word.

_____ 1. communicate

_____ 2. tone

_____ 3. considerate

_____ 4. feedback

_____ 5. constructive criticism

_____ 6. fax machine

_____ 7. body language

a) thoughtful and caring about others

b) showing feelings using your body and your face

c) a way of speaking that shows a certain feeling

d) tips that help someone or something improve

e) a machine that sends and receives information on paper using a phone line

f) information people give you about your work

g) to share thoughts, feelings, and ideas with others

Fill in the blank in each sentence with a word from the box.

regret	atmosphere	clients
criticize	attitude	answering machine
apologize	assist	

8. Mrs. Hixson knew she had to _____ because she was late to the party.

9. When Pete has to _____ Manuel, he uses a friendly tone of voice.

10. Customers feel they are well taken care of when you approach them with a good _____ .

11. The people who use your business are your _____.

12. Manuel and his coworkers enjoy working at Pete's because the _____ is relaxed and professional.

13. Every morning Manuel checks the _____ for messages.

14. If he didn't correct the mistake right away, he knew he would _____ it.

15. When Mrs. Hixson needed help, Manuel was happy to _____ her.

II. Main Ideas

Circle the letter of the correct answer.

16. It is important to communicate well with customers because
    a) you want to give them what they want.
    b) the customers have no other place to go.
    c) you want to take time off.

17. The telephone at work can help people
    a) keep in touch with their friends.
    b) receive and send messages about business.
    c) avoid talking directly with clients.

18. Being polite means to
    a) not speak to people unless they speak first.
    b) always say what you think.
    c) be considerate of other people's feelings.

III. What Would You Do?

Write your answers on a separate piece of paper.

19. You work as a receptionist for an accountant. It is tax season, and many people are calling the office. You are already helping a client on the phone, and another phone is ringing. What can you say to the person you are talking to?

20. You are waiting on customers at Mei's Dress Shop. A customer cuts in line. The other customers are annoyed. How can you solve this problem in a polite manner?

21. This morning, Mr. Anson called with an important message for your boss. You forgot to write it down, and you can't remember all the details. What will you do about it?

IV. Solving Workplace Problems

Mrs. Montroy showed Manuel a stained shirt. She said that the stain must be removed. Pete's wasn't able to get the stain out, and Mrs. Montroy is coming in.

22. What should Manuel say to Mrs. Montroy?

_____

_____

23. Why should Manuel keep a helpful, polite attitude?

_____

_____

V. Unit Replay

Go back to the story on page 67. Reread it. Ask yourself again: How would you treat different kinds of people at work? How can different people understand each other? Write your answers on a separate piece of paper.

VI. You . . . and Communicating At Work

Check ✔ the boxes next to the questions you can answer now.
Write an ✗ next to the ones you think you need to work on more.

- ❑ Why do people need to understand one another at work? (Lesson 17)
- ❑ How can you communicate well in the workplace? (Lesson 17)
- ❑ How can telephones be used in the workplace? (Lesson 18)
- ❑ How can you be helpful on the telephone? (Lesson 18)
- ❑ How does it help your company when you are polite? (Lesson 19)
- ❑ How can you ask for help when you need it? (Lesson 20)
- ❑ Why is it important to treat customers well? (Lesson 21)
- ❑ How can you be helpful to a customer? (Lesson 21)
- ❑ How can people give and receive criticism? (Lesson 22)
- ❑ How should you make an apology? (Lesson 23)

If you put an ✗ next to any question, go back and review the lesson.

Unit 5
Getting Along

AT THE TURNER BUILDING SUPPLY COMPANY

Ling's job at the Turner Building Supply Company was to place boxes of nails into large cartons. Several of her coworkers helped. A man named Chip needed some tape. "Hey, give me the tape," he shouted to Ling.

"Gee," thought Ling, "that guy is rude."

Later, Chip and Fred got into a loud argument about the best way to pack the boxes. They were wasting time. Ling was interested in getting the job done. She had other work to do.

At the end of the day, Ling thought to herself: "Sometimes the hardest part of the job is dealing with the different kinds of people here."

What Do You Think?

Why is it sometimes difficult to get along with people? What are some things you do to get along with people?

When people get along with each other, they feel better about their jobs. More work gets done. In this unit, you will learn about:

- Respecting Others
- Resolving Conflict
- Working on a Team
- Working With a Supervisor
- Handling Personal Problems
- Being a Professional
- Working in Today's World

LESSON 24
RESPECTING OTHERS

Lesson Objective

This lesson will help you answer this question:

- **How can coworkers show respect for one another?**

Words to Know:

productive   able to get a lot of work done
appreciate   to be aware that something or someone is valuable

Respect Is Good for Business

In a company that runs well, people do their best to work together. When people show respect for one another, they are more **productive**. When people treat each other with respect, they enjoy their jobs and get more work done. The Turner Building Supply Company has a problem. Several of its workers show little respect for one another. For example, Chip was rude to Ling.

Ways to Show Respect at Work

Here are some ways to show respect to coworkers:

- If you want something, ask for it in a nice way. For example, Chip should have said "*please*" when he asked Ling for the tape.

- If a person does something for you, show that you **appreciate** it. Always say "*thank you.*"

- Do not disturb people when they are working. Chip and Fred should not have talked loudly near Ling.

- If you have to interrupt someone, be sure to apologize.

- Respect people's privacy. If you need to see someone whose door is closed, knock before you enter.

Checkpoint

What are two ways coworkers can show respect for one another?

Think about your answer to this question. Write your answer on a separate piece of paper. Discuss your ideas with a partner. Share your ideas with the class by role-playing with your partner.

WORKPLACE PRACTICE

This activity will give you practice at showing respect to a coworker.

Suppose you work at the Turner Building Supply Company. Chip and Fred are standing nearby. They are talking about a movie. Their voices are loud, and you are having trouble doing your work.

A. Write your answer to the following questions on the lines.

1. What would you say to Chip and Fred?

   _____

2. How should they respond to you?

   _____

B. Choose a partner.

3. Share your answers and discuss other possible answers with your partner.

LESSON REVIEW

Key Words

Complete each sentence with a word from the box.

appreciate	productive

1. When the workers got along, they were more _____.

2. Ling knew that her boss would _____ her hard work.

Thinking About Respecting Others

Circle the sentence that is true.

3. More work gets done when people respect one another.

4. It is not necessary to knock on closed doors.

Workplace Workshop

5. Ling's boss, Ms. Glover, is having a meeting. Ling has to interrupt to tell Ms. Glover about an important visitor. With a classmate, show how Ling and Ms. Glover show respect for one another.

JOB TIP

Never borrow anything from a coworker without asking permission first.

LESSON 25
RESOLVING CONFLICT

This lesson will help you answer these questions:

- **How can conflict be harmful to your job?**
- **How can conflicts be solved in the workplace?**

Words to Know:

conflicts	disagreements
compromise	a way to settle a conflict by having each side agree to give something up in order to get what each wants

Conflict Is Not Good for Business

Conflicts are part of everyday life. Even people who are close will disagree from time to time. Conflicts cannot always be avoided. In fact, to ignore the problem can make the situation worse. The important thing is to know how to handle a conflict so that the relationships or the work can continue. In the workplace, conflicts that are not resolved can become serious problems.

- Conflicts keep people from getting their jobs done.
- Conflicts can cause bad feelings between people.
- As relationships get worse, less work gets done.
- Workers may get sick and have to take time off from work.

The conflict between Chip and Fred was disturbing Ling.

Checkpoint

How can conflict be harmful to your job?

Think about your answer to this question. Write your answer on a separate piece of paper. Discuss your ideas with a partner. Then write these ideas on the chalkboard for the class.

Making Things Better

When a conflict arises, there are several things to keep in mind.

- Take time to calm down before you discuss the problem.

- Make sure that you and the other person agree about what the problem is. The solution may be as simple as clearing up a misunderstanding.

- Everyone who is part of the conflict should be allowed to express their thoughts and feelings.

- It is important to look at the situation, not at the personalities of the people involved.

- Try to understand the other person's needs and point of view.

- See if a **compromise** can be reached. A compromise is a way to settle a conflict by having each side agree to give something up in order to get what each wants.

The Art of Compromise

Sometimes, there is no way to make everyone completely happy. A compromise will help people feel that they have come away with something. It will make it possible for them to get back to work. The following steps can help you reach a compromise:

— It may be a good idea to find someone who is *not* part of the conflict to listen.

— Let each person suggest a solution to the conflict. Talk about the good points and the bad points of each suggestion.

— Try to put together a solution that uses everyone's suggestions.

It's Not Always Easy

Compromising is not always easy. But compromising makes it possible to move on. What can happen if people don't want to compromise?

How can conflicts be solved in the workplace?

Think about your answer to this question. Write your answer on a separate piece of paper. Discuss your ideas with a partner. Then share these ideas with your class.

Checkpoint

WORKPLACE PRACTICE

This activity will give you practice at resolving conflicts.

Suppose that you and Chip work together at Turner Building Supply Company. A conflict has come up. You think that Chip is taking too many breaks. Because of that, you are doing more than your share of the work. Think about how you might solve the conflict.

A. Write your answers to the following questions on the lines.

　　1. What is the conflict?

　　　　_____

　　　　_____

　　　　_____

　　2. What are two problems that the conflict causes?

　　　　_____

　　　　_____

　　3. How could the conflict be resolved?

　　　　_____

　　　　_____

　　　　_____

　　4. How would things in the workplace change after you and Chip resolved the conflict?

　　　　_____

　　　　_____

　　　　_____

B. Choose a partner. You and your partner discuss your solutions.

　　5. Does your partner have another solution? On the lines below, add other possible solutions.

　　　　_____

　　　　_____

　　　　_____

　　　　_____

LESSON REVIEW

Key Words and Ideas

Complete each sentence with a word from the box.

conflicts	compromise

1. Disagreements are also called _____.

2. A _____ is a way to settle a conflict by having each side agree to give something up.

Write the answers to the following questions on the lines.

3. If conflict is not resolved in the workplace, what can happen?

_____

4. How can misunderstandings lead to conflict?

_____

5. Why is a compromise a good way to resolve conflict?

_____

JOB TIP

Try to resolve the conflict as soon as you can. If you ignore the problem it could get worse.

Thinking About Resolving Conflict

Write T next to each statement that is true. Write F next to each statement that is false.

6. Conflict always leads workers to compromise. _____

7. Conflict often stops people from getting their jobs done. _____

8. It is important for people in a conflict to know that express their feelings. _____

9. A good compromise will resolve a conflict. _____

10. A compromise means that one person is right. _____

Workplace Workshop

11. Reread the story on page 91. With three other classmates, role-play the situation at the Turner Building Supply Company. Show how you would handle the problems that Ling, Chip, and Fred are having. Explain how the workplace changes when conflicts are resolved.

LESSON 26
WORKING ON A TEAM

Lesson Objectives

This lesson will help you to answer these questions:

- **What makes a team work well?**
- **What things should a good team member do?**

Words to Know:

common goal	the end result that all team members work toward
cooperate	to work well with others

What Makes a Team Work?

A few heads and hands working together often perform better than a person working alone. A team is a group of people who work together. The members of a team work together for a **common goal**. Every member of the team tries to get the job done.

Teams get things done when people **cooperate**. On a successful team, no one person has all the ideas or does all the work. Some members may do certain things better than others. But everyone has a valuable job to do as part of the team.

When Ling and her team work together, they cooperate and share their ideas. When they resolve their conflicts, they are able to use their energy to do their jobs.

A lot of work gets done when Ling, Fred, and Chip cooperate with each other.

Checkpoint

What makes a team work well?

Think about your answer to this question. Write your answer on a separate piece of paper. Discuss your ideas with a partner. Make a poster that shows teams at work, and display it for the class.

Belonging to a Team

There are many teams in your community. People work together to keep a building clean, to run a store, or to plan an event. Everyone has a job to do. The team can reach its goal when all the team members do their jobs well.

HOW YOU CAN BE A GOOD **TEAM MEMBER**

DO

- help other team members if they need it.
- treat members as you would like to be treated.
- listen to the ideas of others.
- keep the team's goal in mind.

DON'T

- think your job is more important than anyone else's.
- talk about members to others.
- ignore the suggestions of others.

HOW YOU CAN BE A GOOD **TEAM LEADER**

DO

- treat all members equally.
- give directions clearly.
- respect the feelings of your workers.
- encourage members to discuss their problems.

DON'T

- act "bossy."
- wait a long time to correct mistakes.
- expect everything to be perfect.
- be afraid to try new methods.

It's Not Always Easy

Some people are not easy to work with. Sometimes talking to the person can help. If the problem continues, you may need to discuss it with your boss. Why should you talk to your boss?

What are three things that a good team member should do?

Think about your answer to this question. Write your answer on a separate piece of paper. Discuss your ideas with a partner and present them to the class.

Checkpoint

WORKPLACE PRACTICE

This activity will give you practice at working on a team.

Suppose you and your coworkers work in a clothing store. Winter is coming. Your boss wants your team to fix up the store window to show the winter items that are sold.

A. Write your answers to the following questions on the lines.

1. What comes to mind when you think of winter?

_____

_____

2. What should be included in a store window for winter?

_____

_____

B. Form a team with a small group of classmates.

3. Together with your teammates, discuss all of your ideas for the store. Which ideas are best? Write them on the lines.

_____

_____

4. What are the different jobs? Who will do them? List the jobs that need to be done. Decide with team members who will do each job. (There is not a lot of money to spend, but scenery and props can be made or drawn.)

Task	Person
_____	_____
_____	_____
_____	_____
_____	_____
_____	_____

LESSON REVIEW

Key Words and Ideas

Write the letter of the correct definition for each word.

1. _____ cooperate
2. _____ common goal

a) to work well with others

b) the end result that every team member works toward

Write the answers to the following question on the lines.

3. What do you look for in a good team member? List two things in your answer.

_____

_____

Thinking About Working on a Team

Circle the letter of the correct answer.

4. Which of the following is *not* a team?

   a) a ship's crew
   b) actors in a play
   c) a solo pianist
   d) a family

5. A good team member should

   a) take control.
   b) help other members.
   c) pay no attention to others.
   d) have the most important job.

6. Which of the following things should a team leader do?

   a) treat everyone equally
   b) criticize members often
   c) talk about other team members
   d) listen to only some team members

JOB TIP

Members of a good team learn from their mistakes. They try to correct them for the next time.

Workplace Workshop

7. Chip is leaving the Turner Building Supply Company for another job. His coworkers are having a party to say good-bye. Form a planning team with a few classmates. Choose a team leader who will assign tasks. People will be needed to make decisions about decorations, snacks, and the place for the party.

LESSON 27
WORKING WITH A SUPERVISOR

This lesson will help you answer this question:

- **How can you get along well with your supervisor?**

Words to Know:

supervisor	someone who watches over and directs the work of another person
courtesy	behaving in a way that shows good manners and respect for others

A Most Important Relationship

Whenever Ling has a question about her job, she speaks to her **supervisor**. A supervisor is an important person in the workplace. Supervisors watch how well you are doing your job. They are the people to talk to about time off, raises, or other important matters. They are the ones to go to with any questions about your job. When you have a problem or complaint about work, talk to your supervisor.

These points will help you get along with your supervisor:

- Always treat your supervisor with *courtesy*. Courtesy is behaving in a way that shows good manners and respect.

- If you have extra time, offer to help your supervisor. Don't wait until your supervisor notices that you have nothing to do.

- Accept criticism from your supervisor calmly. It is part of your supervisor's job to tell workers how they are doing. Your supervisor's comments can help you improve your work.

- When your supervisor asks you to do a task, find out when it should be completed. Let your supervisor know if it is taking longer than expected.

How can you get along well with your supervisor?

Think about your answer to this question. Write your answer on a separate piece of paper. Discuss your ideas with a partner. Then share these ideas with the class.

WORKPLACE PRACTICE

This activity will help you practice working with a supervisor.

Suppose you want to ask your supervisor for vacation time.

A. Write your answers to the following questions on the lines.

1. What would you say to your supervisor?

_____

2. What would you say if your supervisor said "no"?

_____

B. Choose a partner. Take turns role-playing this activity with your partner.

LESSON REVIEW

Key Words

Draw a line from the word to its corrrect definition.

1. courtesy   a) someone who watches over and directs the work of another person

2. supervisor   b) behaving in a way that shows good manners and respect

Thinking About Working With a Supervisor

Circle the letter of the correct answer.

3. If you have some free time at work you should

    a) leave the workplace for 10 minutes.

    b) make a telephone call to a friend.

    c) offer to help your supervisor.

Workplace Workshop

4. With a group, go to a school employee who has the duties of a supervisor. Ask questions about the job. Interview a person who works for the supervisor. Share the results with the class.

JOB TIP

No matter how difficult your supervisor is, never be rude. Remember, your supervisor has something to say about your raises.

LESSON 28
HANDLING PERSONAL PROBLEMS

This lesson will help you answer this question:

- **How can you handle personal problems *and* a job?**

Words to Know:

personal	something that is private
appropriate	suitable at the time

Personal Problems and the Workplace

Everyone has problems that are **personal**. It is best to leave these problems at home. They do not belong in the workplace. Employers expect workers to do their job. Personal problems may seem important at the time, but it is **appropriate** to discuss them only after business hours.

Ling has met many new people at her job. She knows, however, that she has to keep her personal life out of the workplace. Ling understands that the purpose of a job is to perform her tasks. She made a list of rules for herself:

1. When at work, do not discuss personal problems.

2. With new friends at work, discuss personal matters on breaks and at lunch.

3. Never talk to friends on the phone about private things. Wait until after work.

How can you handle personal problems *and* a job?

Think about your answer to this question. Write your answer on a separate piece of paper. Discuss your ideas with a partner. Then write your ideas in a paragraph and read it to the class.

WORKPLACE PRACTICE

This activity will help you to handle personal matters and a job.

Suppose you are standing by the water cooler at work. Phil, a coworker, joins you.

A. Read what Phil says.

"Hey, how's it going? Listen to this great vacation I'm planning. I know we have to finish the shipment by 3:00, but this is exciting. It will take just a few minutes to tell you."

B. Choose a partner. Discuss with your partner what you should do.

LESSON REVIEW

Key Words

Complete each sentence with a word from the box.

| personal   appropriate |

1. I know it's not a good idea to discuss _____ matters on the job.

2. After work is an _____ time to talk to my friends about problems with my boyfriend.

Thinking About Handling Personal Problems

Circle the letter of the correct answer.

3. A good reason not to discuss personal problems at work is:
   a) nobody cares.
   b) your problems aren't serious.
   c) your time there is for working.

Workplace Workshop

4. Discuss as a class the difficulties one might have in keeping personal problems out of the workplace. What types of personal problems should never be brought to the workplace? What types of problems might you want to share with a supervisor or coworker?

JOB TIP

There may be a time when a personal problem is harming your work. If that happens, talk to your supervisor. Your supervisor may be able to suggest someone in your company to help you.

LESSON 29
BEING A PROFESSIONAL

This lesson will help you answer this question:

- **How can you be a professional at work?**

Words to Know:

gossip	to talk about people's personal lives
professional	a person who acts in a responsible and businesslike way
boundaries	limits

Separating Work and Private Life

One day Ling was talking to Diana, a coworker. Diana began to **gossip** about another coworker. To gossip is to talk about people's personal lives. It can make people angry at each other. It is not good for the workplace.

Ling explained to Diana that she didn't like to gossip. Most of the stories weren't true. And besides, it was important to respect the privacy of the people they worked with. Diana thought about it and agreed. She said she'd try to be more **professional**. Being a professional is to act in a responsible and businesslike way.

People who are professionals are aware of **boundaries**, or limits. It is important to respect the boundaries between work and private life. The following list will help you do this.

- You should not gossip about others.
- You should not do things that would cause others to gossip about you.
- Dating coworkers is not a good idea. Dating coworkers can cause personal problems that may affect your work.
- Don't discuss salaries or other private matters.

How can you be a professional at work?

Think about your answer to this question. Write your answer on a separate piece of paper. Discuss your ideas with a partner. Then share your ideas with the class.

WORKPLACE PRACTICE

This activity will help you practice to be a professional.

Suppose that you work at a bicycle shop. One of your coworkers, Charley, is always gossiping.

A. Write your answer to the following question on the lines.

1. Why is it harmful to gossip about coworkers?

_____

_____

B. Choose a partner.

2. With your partner, decide what to say to Charley to get him to stop gossiping.

LESSON REVIEW

Key Words

Complete each sentence with a word from the box.

gossip	professional	boundaries

1. Limits are types of _____ .

2. To talk about people's personal lives is to _____ .

3. To be a _____ is to act in a businesslike way.

Thinking About Being a Professional

Circle the sentence that is true.

4. If you are a professional, people will gossip about you.

5. You should avoid dating your coworkers.

Workplace Workshop

6. Suppose a coworker tells you that your boss is dating someone in your office. Have a class discussion about what you should do with this information and why.

JOB TIP

If someone starts to gossip about a coworker, make sure you don't spread what you heard.

LESSON 30
WORKING IN TODAY'S WORLD

This lesson will help you answer these questions:

- **How is diversity good for the workplace?**
- **How can you handle prejudice in the workplace?**

Words to Know:

diversity	difference, variety
international	made up of people from different nations
prejudice	an opinion of other people that is not based on facts

Today's World

Ling works with many different people. They are different ages, they are of different races, they come from different countries, they have different sets of beliefs, they have different abilities. The **diversity** of the Turner Building Supply Company reflects the many differences of the people in the United States today.

Ling has discovered that such diversity can be good. With diversity, people learn from one another's experience and skills. Also, more and more countries are doing business with one another. This **international** business makes different people's languages and experiences valuable.

People usually find they are more alike than different.

How is diversity good for the workplace?

Think about your answer to this question. Write your answer on a separate piece of paper. Discuss your ideas with a partner. Then write your ideas in your journal or notebook.

What Is Prejudice?

Sometimes people develop an opinion about someone else—or about a group of people—that is not based on fact. This type of opinion is called **prejudice**.

Prejudice is unfair and harmful. It is stupid. It is not based on information. Prejudice often is caused by fear. It comes from a fear of people who are different.

Prejudice prevents people from getting jobs. It keeps them from doing what they can do. It stops people from getting ahead.

How to Get Rid of Prejudice

There are two good ways to get rid of prejudice. The first way is to be careful of your own behavior. The second way is to do the right thing if someone else shows prejudice. Read the statements below.

How to Behave

— Keep an open mind when you meet new people.

— Treat people with equal respect.

— Try to include people in your life who are different from you.

What to Do if Someone Shows Prejudice

— Think about if it really was prejudice. Make sure you have not misunderstood your coworker.

— If a customer expresses prejudice, simply walk away.

— If a coworker expresses a prejudice, tell him or her that you do not permit such behavior. Talk with a supervisor if it continues. If your supervisor is the problem, try to speak to someone higher up.

It's Not Always Easy

Everyone makes mistakes. If you ever say something that hurts someone, you need to apologize. Why is it important to say that you are sorry?

How can you handle prejudice in the workplace?

Think about your answer to this question. Write your answer on a separate piece of paper. Discuss your ideas with a partner. Then write your ideas on a chart.

Checkpoint

WORKPLACE PRACTICE

This activity will help you understand how diversity can be good for the workplace.

Think of the different jobs that people have at your school. There are teachers, custodians, cafeteria workers, office workers, and others. Prepare an interview with one of these people.

A. Use the following questions. Write the answers on the lines.

1. Your family originally came from which country or countries?

   _____

2. What languages are spoken in your family?

   _____

3. What is your job at the school?

   _____

4. What skills do you bring to your job?

   _____

5. What would happen at school if you didn't do your job?

   _____

B. Choose a partner.

6. Discuss how diversity is good for your school. Write your ideas on the lines.

   _____

   _____

   _____

7. With your partner, think of ways in which diversity has added to your life. Think about the music you listen to and the foods that you eat. Write your ideas on the lines.

   _____

   _____

   _____

LESSON REVIEW

Key Words and Ideas

Complete each sentence with a word from the box.

Diversity	International	Prejudice

1. _____ means made up of people from different nations.

2. _____ is an opinion of other people that is not based on facts.

3. _____ means difference or variety.

Write the answer to the following questions on the lines.

4. How does prejudice harm the workplace?

_____

5. In what ways is diversity good for the workplace?

_____

Thinking About Working in Today's World

Circle the letter of the correct answer.

6. People can learn different skills from each other when
   a) everyone is the same.
   b) everyone is prejudiced.
   c) there is diversity in the workplace.
   d) people make the same salary.

7. A good way to prevent prejudice is to:
   a) treat everyone with equal respect.
   b) tell some people that they are better than anyone else.
   c) form an opinion without facts.
   d) not ask questions.

Workplace Workshop

8. Work with your class to write a letter to the mayor of your town. Explain how the diversity of people who live there has been good for the community.

Unit 5 Review
G e t t i n g   A l o n g

In this unit you learned about:

- **Respecting Others**
- **Resolving Conflict**
- **Working on a Team**
- **Working With a Supervisor**
- **Handling Personal Problems**
- **Being a Professional**
- **Working in Today's World**

I. Vocabulary

A. Write the letter of the correct definition next to each word.

_____ 1. diversity

_____ 2. international

_____ 3. common goal

_____ 4. gossip

_____ 5. productive

_____ 6. courtesy

_____ 7. appreciate

_____ 8. personal

_____ 9. appropriate

a) to be aware that something or someone is valuable

b) something that is private

c) difference, variety

d) made up of people from different nations

e) the end result that all team members work toward

f) to talk about people's personal lives

g) suitable at the time

h) able to get a lot of work done

i) behaving in a way that shows good manners and respect for others

B. Complete each sentence with a word from the box.

conflicts	cooperate	boundaries
supervisor	prejudice	
compromise	professional	

10. Ling avoids _____ or disagreements with other workers.

11. Ling believes that to be a _____, she has to be on time and be responsible.

12. Iris and Marcus decided to _____ by paying one dollar each to settle their argument.

13. Ling went to her _____ when she had a problem with her work.

14. Ling knows it's important to _____ or work well with others.

15. Each worker knows the _____ or limits of his or her job.

16. To have a _____ is to have an opinion of other people that is not based on facts.

II. Main Ideas

Circle the letter of the correct answer.

17. The purpose of the workplace is to

    a) resolve conflicts.   **c)** make friends.

    b) get the job done.

18. One way to respect the boundaries between work and private life is to

    a) gossip about others.   **c)** discuss salaries or other private matters.

    b) avoid dating coworkers.

III. What Would You Do?

Write your answers to the following questions on the lines.

19. You work in an office. You receive a phone call saying that you are needed at home. You need permission from your boss to leave the office. However, the boss is in her office and her door is closed. What should you do?

    _____

    _____

20. Suppose that you are part of a team that cleans houses in your neighorhood. Write two things good team members should do.

    _____

    _____

21. A coworker comes over to gossip about your boss. What should you say to your coworker?

    _____

    _____

IV. Solving Workplace Problems

Read the paragraph and answer the questions on the lines.

Mark and Damon work at a hardware store. Their boss asked them to unpack some boxes of tools by the afternoon. Mark wants to eat lunch from 12 to 1 o'clock and then unpack the boxes. Damon wants to eat lunch from 1 to 2 o'clock and then unpack the boxes after that.

23. How can Mark and Damon compromise?

   _____

24. How would this be a good solution to the problem?

   _____

V. Unit Replay

Go back to the story on page 91. Reread it. Ask yourself again: Why is it sometimes difficult to get along with people? What are some things you do to get along with people? Write your answers on a separate piece of paper.

VI. You . . . and Getting Along

Check ✔ the boxes next to the questions you can answer now.
Write an ✗ next to the ones you think you need to work on more.

- ☐ How can coworkers show respect for one another? (Lesson 24)
- ☐ How can conflict be harmful to your job? (Lesson 25)
- ☐ How can conflicts be solved in the workplace? (Lesson 25)
- ☐ What makes a team work well? (Lesson 26)
- ☐ What things should a good team member do? (Lesson 26)
- ☐ How can you get along well with your supervisor? (Lesson 27)
- ☐ How can you handle personal problems and a job? (Lesson 28)
- ☐ How can you be a professional at work? (Lesson 29)
- ☐ How is diversity good for the workplace? (Lesson 30)
- ☐ How can you handle prejudice in the workplace? (Lesson 30)

If you put an ✗ next to any question, go back and review the lesson.

Unit 6
Meeting
Challenges

CHANGES AT THE BARTON TRAVEL AGENCY

Dennis's workplace — the Barton Travel Agency — was a mess. Workers were putting in new equipment.

Dennis thought to himself: "The new equipment will make it easier to do business. We will now have a better system to sell tickets. Keeping records will be simpler."

But another thought worried him. "Will I be able to work the new equipment?" He then said to himself, "There was a time when I couldn't work the old machine either. But I learned."

Dennis realized he had to be willing to make changes.

What Do You Think?

How do you deal with change? What kind of challenges have you met in your life?

Change is an important part of the workplace. In this unit, you will learn about:

- Entering the Changing Workplace
- Using Computers
- Learning Skills for the Job
- Protecting Yourself at Work
- Dealing With Harassment
- Relieving Job Stress
- Losing a Job

LESSON 31
ENTERING THE CHANGING WORKPLACE

Lesson Objective

This lesson will help you answer this question:

- **How has the workplace changed in recent years?**

Words to Know:

flexible schedules	working hours that are fixed to meet people's changing needs
technology	the use of science to do practical things

Times of Change

In today's workplace, **flexible schedules** have become common. These schedules meet the needs of many of today's workers. Among the workers of today are high school students, single parents, and new parents. Anna, one of Dennis's coworkers, has two young children. The agency has fixed her schedule so that she can be home after school.

Important Skills

Changes may take place, but basic skills continue to be important.

> — Reading, writing, and math are still important.
> — Thinking skills, such as making decisions, will always be needed in the workplace.
> — Communication skills will always be useful.
> — Social skills are always important.

Basic skills are important. But new skills are also important in the workplace today. A demand for new skills has been brought about by **technology**. Technology has brought computers into the workplace.

More and more, computers are used to create, organize, store, and exchange information. Many jobs require computer skills. You will learn more about computers in the next lesson.

Checkpoint

How has the workplace changed in recent years?

Think about your answer to this question. Write your answer on a separate piece of paper. Discuss your ideas with a partner. Then make a list of your ideas and read it to the class.

WORKPLACE PRACTICE

This activity will give you practice at understanding the changing workplace.

A. Read the paragraph.

José has recently been hired at the Barton Travel Agency. José goes to school Mondays, Wednesdays, and Fridays from 9:00 A.M. to 1:00 P.M. He has a computer course on Tuesdays from 3:00 P.M. to 5:00 P.M. On Saturdays, he coaches a soccer team. The agency is open every day from 10:00 A.M. to 6:00 A.M. except Sunday.

B. With a partner, make a work schedule for José.

On a separate piece of paper, enter the hours and the days José could work. He wants to work 20 hours a week.

LESSON REVIEW

Key Words

Complete each sentence with a word from the box.

> technology   flexible schedules

1. Dennis wanted to learn the new _____ .

2. The agency introduced _____ to meet the needs of many workers.

Thinking About the Changing Workplace

Circle the correct answer.

3. In the workplace, most people

   a) have no needs.   **c)** have special needs.

   b) work part-time.

Workplace Workshop

4. Work with a partner to choose a type of work. Then find a person in this business and ask him or her the following questions:

   • How is technology changing in your field?

   • What new skills do you think people in your field will need in the next five to ten years?

JOB TIP

Knowing more than one language can help you in the changing workplace.

LESSON 32
USING COMPUTERS

This lesson will help you answer these questions:

- **How do computers help us organize information?**
- **How do computers help us communicate information?**

Words to Know:

Internet	the system that connects millions of different kinds of computers around the world
e-mail	electronic mail by which messages can be sent by computer
on-line	connected to a computer network

How Computers Help Organize Information

At the Barton Travel Agency, Dennis uses a computer to organize the information he needs to serve his clients.

Dennis uses his computer to get the information he needs.

Computers in the workplace have many uses. Some of them are:

- storing information about sales of a company's products
- organizing information about the company's profits
- keeping track of what has to be ordered
- keeping records of workers and their employment histories
- keeping records of customers and clients
- keeping records of expenses

How do computers help people organize information in the workplace?

Think about your answer. Write your answer on a separate piece of paper. Discuss your ideas with a partner. Then share these ideas with your class.

How Computers Communicate Information

Today, millions of people can share information with one another. The **Internet** makes this possible. The Internet is a system that connects individual computers around the world.

At the Barton Travel Agency, the agents use the Internet for travel information. They find out about schedules, fares, and hotels. They can see what's available and then book reservations for their clients.

Their computers make it possible for people at the agency to communicate through **e-mail**. (The "e" stands for "electronic" — which means that the information is sent through the computer.)

Here's a note card that helps Dennis remember the ways he can use his computer.

- Use the Internet to go "on-line" to find information about airlines, hotels, and car rentals.

- Use e-mail to communicate with clients and companies.

- Use the Internet to find Web sites for information about weather, for articles about various places, and for news about different parts of the world.

- Use the Internet for information in dictionaries, encyclopedias, phone books, and other reference materials. Remember, the Internet is connected to thousands of libraries around the world.

It's Not Always Easy

At first it may be difficult to work with computers. If you are having trouble, find out if there is a course you can take. Why is it a good idea to improve your computer skills?

How do computers help us communicate information?

Think about your answer to this question. Write your answer on a separate piece of paper. Discuss your ideas with a partner. Then make a list that combines your ideas and read it to the class.

Checkpoint

WORKPLACE PRACTICE

This activity will help you think about ways to use computers.

In the 1950s, computers were used mainly by the military. They were the size of a large room. Today, they are used by millions of homes and businesses. And they are small enough to fit on a desk, on a lap, or even in a pocket. Think about how they could help you organize and communicate information in your own life.

A. Write your answers to the following questions on the lines.

1. How could a computer help you organize information at school?

   _____

   _____

2. How could a computer help you organize information at home?

   _____

   _____

3. How could a computer help you communicate information at school?

   _____

   _____

4. How could a computer help you communicate information at home?

   _____

   _____

B. Choose a partner.

5. Discuss your answers to the above questions with your partner. Write down anything important that you want to add.

   _____

   _____

   _____

LESSON REVIEW

Key Words and Ideas

Complete each sentence with a word from the box.

on-line	Internet	e-mail

1. Dennis used the _____ to see if there were any airline tickets.

2. When you are connected to a computer network, you are

   _____ .

3. He sent a message by _____ to wish her a good trip.

Write the answers to the following questions on the lines.

4. How do computers help us organize information?

   _____

   _____

5. What are ways that computers help us communicate information?

   _____

   _____

Thinking About Using Computers

Circle the letter of the correct answer.

6. Dennis used e-mail mostly to

   a) send messages to other people.   c) take phone messages.

   b) organize records in folders.

Workplace Workshop

7. Dennis has a new client named Mrs. Finley. She has asked him to create a "dream vacation" for her and her family. She has a husband and two daughters, ages 12 and 10. Work with a partner. Write down how you would go about planning the trip. Note the ways in which you could use a computer.

LESSON 33
LEARNING SKILLS FOR THE JOB

This lesson will help you answer this question:

- **How can you get the skills you need for your job?**

Words to Know:

on-the-job training	learning a job while working
trainee	someone who is learning how to do a job

Learning While You Work

There are several ways to learn the skills you need on your job. One way is to learn as you work. This is called **on-the-job training**. To get on-the-job training, someone may explain the work to you. Or, you could watch others do the job. In either case, it is important to pay close attention. Be sure to ask questions if anything is unclear.

Improving Your Skills

Sometimes jobs change. New skills are needed. When this happens, what can you do? Here are a few things:

— Talk to your supervisor or boss about learning new skills. This will show that you have an interest in learning more about the job.

— Find out if there are classes to take. For instance, if you want to learn about using a computer, look for courses on computer skills.

— Some coworkers may have the skill that you want. If so, ask them how they learned what they know. Perhaps they can teach the skill to you.

— Wherever you are learning, remember to take notes. You may want to look at them in the future.

How can you get the skills you need for your job?

Think about your answer to this question. Write your answer on a separate piece of paper. Discuss your ideas with a partner. Then share them with the class.

WORKPLACE PRACTICE

This activity will give you practice at learning about skills for a job.

Suppose you and a partner are working at the Barton Travel Agency. One of you will be the trainer and the other the **trainee**, or the person who is learning a new job. The trainer is showing the new employee around the office and explaining what is expected.

A. Role-play a training session. Use the following questions.

- What are the phone numbers I need to have for my job?
- Who do I go to if I have a question about the work?
- What questions do I ask a client to find out everything I need to know?

B. Add any other questions that you think may be useful.

LESSON REVIEW

Key Words

Complete each sentence with a word from the box.

on-the-job training	trainee

1. Dennis had _____. His supervisor showed him how to issue tickets to customers.

2. Someone who is learning a new job is called a _____.

Thinking About Learning Skills for the Job

Circle the letter of the correct answer.

3. Which of the following is a good way to get on-the-job training?

   a) talk to your cousin   c) ask your boss to explain things

   b) tell your boss that you know how everything works

Workplace Workshop

4. With a group, choose 10 want ads from a newspaper and list the skills required for the jobs.

JOB TIP

Local colleges, libraries, and community centers often have courses that would help you at work. You can call and ask them to send you information.

LESSON 34
PROTECTING YOURSELF AT WORK

This lesson will help you answer these questions:

- **How are workers' rights protected?**
- **How can you make sure your workplace is safe?**

Words to Know:

discrimination	the treatment of some people better than others for an unfair reason
hazards	risks or dangers

Your Rights on the Job

There are laws in the United States that protect workers.

There is a minimum-wage law. This law sets the least amount of money that an employer can pay an employee.

There are also laws that protect workers from **discrimination**. Companies cannot keep a person from being hired because of the person's race, color, religion, gender, age, or arrest record.

The Americans with Disabilities Act protects people with disabilities. The law requires employers to make it possible for people who are disabled to work at their jobs.

Dennis likes working for a company that treats employees fairly.

Checkpoint

How are workers' rights protected?

Think about your answer. Write it on a separate piece of paper. Discuss your ideas with a partner and share them with the class.

Safety at Work

Your company is responsible for protecting your rights. It is also responsible for protecting your safety. Make sure that your workplace is a safe place for you to be. People can face many **hazards**, or dangers, on their jobs. Here are ways to be safe at work.

CHEMICALS AND SAFETY

— Make sure that all chemicals are labeled and stored correctly.

— All chemicals should be thrown out in the proper way.

— Employees should wear gloves, masks, and other equipment when working with chemicals.

ELECTRICITY AND SAFETY

— Electrical wires should not be worn or broken.

— All plugs should fit tightly. There should not be too many plugs in one socket.

— Make sure electrical products are not near water.

— Only trained professionals should fix electrical problems.

FIRE AND SAFETY

— Know where fire exits are located.

— Find out if there is a smoke detector. This is a device that gives off a warning sound when smoke is around.

— Notice where the fire extinguishers are. A fire extinguisher is a device that is used to spray chemicals on a fire to put it out.

— Make sure there is a plan to get out of the building in case of fire.

How can you make sure your workplace is safe?
Think about your answer to this question. Write your answer on a separate piece of paper. Discuss your ideas with a partner. Make a poster that illustrates these ideas.

Checkpoint

WORKPLACE PRACTICE

This activity will help you think about ways to protect yourself at work.

Read each situation below and then answer the questions on the lines.

1. Julia works for a company that refinishes furniture. She and the other employees work around dangerous paints and chemicals. They also spend a lot of time sanding wood and old paint. The company does not give them masks or gloves. What should they do?

   _____

   _____

   _____

2. Jason is 55 years old and has worked as a loan officer for five years. He has very good references. He answers a newspaper ad for a job as a loan officer. He is told that he does not have enough experience. The next day he learns that the job was given to a 21-year-old man who has no work experience. Do you think Jason may be a victim of discrimination? What do you think he should do?

   _____

   _____

   _____

3. Harriet works in a factory that makes blouses. To make sure that the factory has proper safety controls in case of fire, what should she do?

   _____

   _____

   _____

4. Stacey was hired to work on a fishing boat. When she was hired, she did not discuss how much the job paid. She thought the job would pay $7.00 an hour. When she got her check, she discovered that she was being paid $5.00 an hour. What should Stacey do?

   _____

   _____

   _____

LESSON REVIEW

Key Words and Ideas

Write the word next to the matching definition.

> hazards   discrimination

1. the unfair treatment of a person _____

2. dangers _____

Write the answer to the following question on the line.

3. How can people at work make sure they are safe from
   chemical hazards?

   _____

Thinking About Protecting Yourself at Work

Circle the letter of the correct answer.

4. Discrimination is wrong because

   a) all people deserve to be treated fairly.

   b) everyone can do the same things.

   c) people can't change.

5. When you begin a job, you should know

   a) what the minimum wage is.

   b) the names of every other employee.

   c) how to speak several languages.

Circle the sentence that is true.

6. Laws protect you against discrimination in the workplace.

7. If you are working in a dangerous situation, there is nothing
   you can do.

Workplace Workshop

8. Work in small groups. Make a poster that illustrates a safe workplace.
   Indicate all the things that workers should be careful about. Include
   the ways in which they should make sure their workplace is free
   of hazards.

JOB TIP

If you feel that you have been treated unfairly at work, speak to your supervisor, to the company's Department of Human Resources, or to a lawyer. Discrimination is against the law!

LESSON 35
DEALING WITH HARASSMENT

Lesson Objective

This lesson will help you answer this question:

- **What can you do to handle harassment?**

Words to Know:

harassment	the act of being annoyed again and again
threat	an expression that hints that punishment or harm will follow

Harassment and the Workplace

Harassment is the act of being annoyed again and again. Below is a list of ways you might be harassed in the workplace:

- A request to get involved with someone in exchange for something else, such as pay, gifts, promotion, or other special favors.

- A **threat**, such as, "If you don't do this, I'll fire you."

- Any comments or behavior about body parts that makes you uncomfortable. Jokes or stories that make you uncomfortable.

- A display of materials, such as magazines, cartoons, calendars, or videos that makes you uncomfortable.

Here are some things to do if you think that you are the victim of harassment:

— Talk to the person. He or she may not realize how you feel.

— If that doesn't work, talk to your supervisor.

— If your supervisor is the problem, speak with another person or that person's supervisor.

Checkpoint

What can you do to handle harassment?

Think about your answer to this question. Write your answer on a separate piece of paper. Discuss your ideas with a partner and make a list of them.

WORKPLACE PRACTICE

This activity will give you practice at dealing with harassment.

A. Write your answer to the following questions on the lines.

1. A coworker keeps asking you for a date. It is annoying. What would you say to that person?

    _____

2. The coworker says nothing wrong has happened. The harassment continues. What would you do then?

    _____

B. Choose a partner. Discuss your answers.

LESSON REVIEW

Key Words and Ideas

Underline the word in parentheses that correctly completes each sentence.

1. It is a (threat résumé) when someone hints that punishment or harm will follow.

2. The act of being annoyed again and again is (a hazard, harassment).

Thinking About Dealing with Harassment

Circle the letter of the correct answer.

3. Which of the following is an example of harassment?

    a) giving a worker a raise in salary

    b) telling someone that she will be hired if she goes on a date

    c) asking a coworker to have lunch in the cafeteria

Workplace Workshop

4. Divide into groups. Each group should work together to describe situations that they think are examples of harassment. The group can work together to make a handbook with information about different types of harassment.

It's Not Always Easy

Harassment is usually difficult to talk about. But it's important to talk to someone you trust. A family member or a counselor is a good choice. Why is it important to tell someone?

LESSON 36
RELIEVING JOB STRESS

Lesson Objective

This lesson will help you answer this question:

- **What are some ways to handle stress on the job?**

Words to Know:

stress	worry, strain, or pressure
concentrate	pay close attention

Stress at Work

When Dennis has **stress**, he feels worried and strained. Here are some signs of his job stress:

- He can't **concentrate** on his task. His mind wanders.
- He has difficulty sleeping.
- He has headaches or stomachaches.
- His eating habits change. He may eat too much or too little.

There are ways to handle stress on the job. These tips come from the Barton Travel Agency's employee handbook:

- **Relax. Take several slow, deep breaths.**

- **Raise your arms over your head. Slowly lower them and bring them back up. Do this a few times.**

- **Take a short walk. If you can't go outside, walk in the hall.**

- **Have a healthful snack.**

- **Talk to your supervisor. Perhaps your supervisor can help.**

Checkpoint

What are some ways to handle stress on the job?

Think about your answer to this question. Write your answer on a separate piece of paper. Discuss your ideas with a partner. Then show the class some ways to reduce stress on the job.

WORKPLACE PRACTICE

This activity will give you practice at handling stress.

A. Write your answer to the following questions on the lines.

1. You work at the supermarket. All the items for aisle four have to be unpacked by noon the next day. You are having trouble falling asleep. What should you do?

   _____

   _____

2. Your coworker Steve complains to you that he is worried about his mother's health. He's having trouble concentrating on his work. What do you tell him?

   _____

   _____

B. Choose a partner and discuss your answers with your partner.

LESSON REVIEW

Key Words

Circle the word in parentheses that correctly completes each sentence.

1. When Jennifer had (stress, schedule), she couldn't sleep.

2. As the stress grew, she found it harder to (concentrate, hazard).

Thinking About Relieving Job Stress

Circle the correct answer.

3. One way to handle job stress is to

   a) exercise.   b) hope it goes away.

Workplace Workshop

4. With your class, make a booklet of exercises for people who need to relax. Talk to the physical education teacher in your school. Ask for suggestions for exercises to help people who feel stress.

It's Not Always Easy

Stress makes working difficult to work. If you have stress, do something about it right away. Why is it important to take care of it as soon as you can?

LESSON 37
LOSING A JOB

Lesson Objective

This lesson will help you answer this question:

- **What things can you do if you lose a job?**

Words to Know:

laid off	when workers lose their jobs because a company's needs have changed
severance pay	extra money that an employer gives to laid-off workers
unemployment insurance	government program that provides money to people who have lost their jobs

The Reasons People Lose Jobs

When a company's business is good, there is work to do and jobs to fill. When a company closes or needs fewer workers, employees will be **laid off**. When employees are laid off, they often receive **severance pay**. This is extra money a company gives to employees when they have to let them go.

Sometimes workers lose jobs because an employer is unhappy with their work. They may lack skills, be unable to work, or not arrive on time.

What to Do If You Lose a Job

Here are some things you can do if you lose your job:

- If you are laid off, file for *unemployment insurance.* This may help you pay your bills until you work again.

- Create a new résumé that lists your qualifications and work experience.

- Talk to your friends and coworkers about other job opportunities.

- Look in the want ads for a new job.

Checkpoint

What are two things you can do if you lose a job?
Think about your answer to this question. Write your answer on a separate piece of paper. Discuss your ideas with a partner. Then share these ideas with the class.

WORKPLACE PRACTICE

This activity will help you practice what to do if you lose your job.

A. Read the paragraph, then answer the following questions on the line.

Suppose you are an employee at Butler's Hardware Store. You have been working there one year. Business has been bad, and the owner tells you that she can't afford to keep you on.

1. What will you do for money?

   _____

2. How will you find a new job?

   _____

B. Work with a partner and exchange your answers.

LESSON REVIEW

Key Words

Complete each sentence with a word from the box.

severance pay	unemployment insurance	laid off

1. If you lose a job, you may be able to file for _____.

2. When a company closes, workers may be _____.

3. Some employers provide _____ to workers who are laid off.

Thinking About Losing a Job

Circle the sentence that is true.

4. Everyone gets laid off at some time in their lives.

5. People often get laid off when business is bad.

Workplace Workshop

6. As a class, find out about unemployment in the country and in your area. Call your local unemployment agency or go on-line to find out the percentage of people who are unemployed.

It's Not Always Easy

It's never easy to lose a job. But don't let a lot of time pass before you start to look for another one. Why should you begin your search at once?

Unit 6 Review
Meeting Challenges

In this unit you learned about:

- Entering the Changing Workplace
- Using Computers
- Learning Skills for the Job
- Protecting Yourself at Work
- Dealing With Harassment
- Relieving Job Stress
- Losing a Job

I. Vocabulary

Write the letter of the correct definition next to each word.

_____ 1. Internet

_____ 2. on-line

_____ 3. e-mail

_____ 4. technology

_____ 5. trainee

_____ 6. on-the-job training

_____ 7. hazards

_____ 8. discrimination

a) connected to a computer network

b) learning a job while working

c) a system that connects millions of different kinds of computers around the world

d) risks or dangers

e) electronic mail by which messages can be sent through a computer

f) the use of science to do practical things

g) the treatment of some people better than others for an unfair reason

h) someone who is learning how to do a job

Complete each sentence with a word from the box.

flexible schedules	stress	harassment
severance pay	concentrate	laid off
unemployment insurance	threat	

9. _____ is paid to an employee who has been laid off.

10. When you are feeling _____, you may not be able to do a good job at work.

11. When a company closes, its workers are _____.

12. Lorna felt that she was a victim of _____ and she decided to talk to her supervisor about it.

13. The James Furniture Company has _____ so that its employees can go to school and also work.

14. The government provides _____ to some workers who are laid off.

15. Karla found it hard to _____ when she was worried about her father's health.

16. A _____ is an expression that hints that punishment or harm will follow

II. Main Ideas

Circle the letter of the correct answer.

17. Many new skills are needed in the workplace today because

   a) new people are working.   **c)** basic skills are not needed.

   b) new technology is being used in many businesses.

18. You cannot be paid less than a certain amount on your job because of

   a) minimum wage laws.   **c)** unemployment insurance.

   b) hazards on the job.

19. If you think you have been harassed on a job, you should

   a) report it to a supervisor.   **c)** ignore it and hope it will stop.

   b) quit the job.

III. What Would You Do?

Read the paragraph and answer the questions on the lines.

20. You are working at a company that manufactures children's toys. You have an important deadline coming up. You have been working very long hours. You're not sure you can finish your work on time. Last night you woke up and couldn't sleep. This morning you didn't eat breakfast and had a stomachache. What can you do to ease the situation?

   _____

   _____

21. Your boss has told you that she is sorry but business is slow and they are going to have to let you go. What should you do?

_____

_____

IV. Solving Workplace Problems

On Saturday, Lenny began work as a chef in a hotel kitchen. He wanted to make sure that it was a safe place to work.

Write your answers to the following questions on the lines.

22. What should Lenny do to make sure that he is safe from fire? What should he do to make sure he will escape safely if a fire breaks out?

_____

23. What should Lenny do to make sure that he is safe from electrical hazards?

_____

V. Unit Replay

Go back to the story on page 115. Reread it. Ask yourself again: How do you deal with change? What kind of challenges have you met in your life? Write your answer on a separate piece of paper.

VI. You . . . and Meeting Challenges

Check ✔ the boxes next to the questions you can answer now.
Write an ✗ next to the ones you think you need to work on more.

☐ How has the workplace changed in recent years? (Lesson 31)

☐ How do computers help us organize information? (Lesson 32)

☐ How do computers help us communicate information? (Lesson 32)

☐ How can you get the skills you need for your job? (Lesson 33)

☐ How can you make sure your workplace is safe? (Lesson 34)

☐ How are workers' rights protected? (Lesson 34)

☐ What can you do to handle harassment? (Lesson 35)

☐ What are some ways to handle stress on the job? (Lesson 36)

☐ What things can you do if you lose a job? (Lesson 37)

If you put an ✗ next to any question, go back and review the lesson.

Unit 7
Being Successful

TIME FOR A CHANGE

Tanya has been working at Hank's Luncheonette for two years. It was her first job. There had been a lot to learn. She had to learn the proper knives to use. She had to find out where Hank stored everything. She had to measure the coffee to put into the coffeemaker.

Tanya has received two raises since she started at the restaurant. Hank has been pleased with her work. Tanya knows she has done her job well.

The other day, Tanya heard that Minton's Café is looking for a cook. They want someone to handle the lunchtime meal. Tanya believes that her experience makes her the right person for the job. She feels she is ready for a change. She knows she can take on more responsibility.

Tanya decided to get in touch with Minton's Café the next day.

What Do You Think?

How do you feel about yourself when you know you have done a good job?

Success makes people feel good. In this unit, you will learn about:

- Feeling Sure of Yourself
- Building Self-Esteem
- Moving On

LESSON 38
FEELING SURE OF YOURSELF

This lesson will help you answer this question:

- **How does feeling sure of yourself help you at work?**

Words to Know:

confident	being sure that you can do something well
positive attitude	the expectation that things will turn out well

Becoming Confident

Tanya started working at Hank's Luncheonette two years ago. At the time, she was a little nervous. She started slowly. She made some mistakes. But she did learn, and she has done her job well.

Tanya now feels **confident**. She feels sure about herself and what she can do. Her goal was to do a good job. She has had success.

What Happens When You Feel Confident?

When you feel confident, you have a **positive attitude**. You believe that things will turn out well. Feeling confident is a big help in the workplace. Here are some ways it can help you:

- Employers like to hire people who feel confident and have a positive attitude about their work.

- People who are confident trust themselves.

- Workers who feel confident are open to learning new things.

- Confident people know that if something goes wrong, they'll find a way to fix it.

- Approaching a task with a positive attitude will help you have success.

How does feeling sure of yourself help you at work?

Think about your answer to this question. Write your answer on a separate piece of paper. Discuss your ideas with a partner. Then make a list of these ideas and read it to the class.

WORKPLACE PRACTICE

This activity will give you practice at having a positive attitude.

A. Read the paragraph. Then answer the questions on the lines.

Suppose you have a job at the local bakery. Ray, a coworker, is not confident. Read Ray's statements below. Change his statements so that they show a positive attitude. Make Ray sound confident.

1. "I'll never be able to bake the bread in time."

   _____

2. "That's the worst-tasting cake I've ever eaten!"

   _____

3. "Why should I bother making cookies today? I'm too tired."

   _____

B. Choose a partner. Discuss your statements with each other.

LESSON REVIEW

Key Words

Draw a line from the word to its correct definition.

1. confident   a) being sure that you can do something well

2. positive attitude   b) the expectation that things will turn out well

Thinking About Feeling Sure of Yourself

Circle the sentence that is true.

3. People who are confident have nothing to learn.

4. Employers like to hire people who are confident.

Workplace Workshop

5. Suppose you have a job interview for the mailroom at the town newspaper. You don't have much experience but you believe you can do the job. Role-play with a partner. Try to let the interviewer know that he or she should hire you.

JOB TIP

Be confident, but don't become too self-important. Remember to respect the other people you work with.

LESSON 39
HAVING SELF-ESTEEM

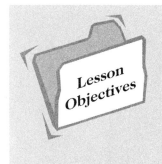
This lesson will help you answer these questions:

- **What is self-esteem?**
- **How can you build self-esteem?**

Words to Know:

self-esteem	the opinion you have of yourself
worth	deserving, having value

What Self-Esteem Is

Tanya has done a good job at Hank's Luncheonette. She has learned a lot and Hank praises her work. She has good **self-esteem**. Self-esteem is the opinion you have of yourself.

Hank tells Tanya that she is doing a good job.

Having a good opinion of yourself is an important goal for everyone. When you have a good opinion of yourself, you have the power to achieve success. You have good self-esteem when you:

- appreciate your own **worth**
- know that your abilities can improve your life
- respect yourself
- do what you think is right
- know that you do your best.

Checkpoint

What is self-esteem?

Think about your answer to this question. Write your answer on a separate piece of paper. Discuss your ideas with a partner. Then write your ideas in your journal or notebook.

Building Self-Esteem

All people have doubts about themselves from time to time. That is not unusual. But good self-esteem will help a person get through a bad time. A person with good self-esteem can always find a way to make things better.

You can build self-esteem in several ways. Here are some ways to do it:

LEARN TO DEAL WITH MISTAKES

— Don't be afraid to make mistakes. Everybody makes mistakes.

— When you make a mistake, admit it.

— Be patient with yourself.

— Learn from your mistakes. Find out what you did wrong.

— Do not let mistakes hold you back. Move on.

MAKE IMPROVEMENTS WHERE NEEDED

— Think about what you want to change about yourself.

— Draw up a plan to make changes.

— Keep track of how you are doing.

— Reward yourself when you have made an improvement.

STAY CONNECTED TO OTHERS

— When you want to meet someone, introduce yourself.

— Offer opinions and suggestions when asked.

— Ask for help and advice from others. This is the best way to avoid mistakes.

— Keep informed about your workplace.

It's Not Always Easy

It's not always easy to change something about yourself right away. Building self-esteem takes time. What things would you like to change about yourself?

How can you build your self-esteem?

Think about your answer to this question. Write your answer on a separate piece of paper. Discuss your ideas with a partner. Then share your ideas with the class.

Checkpoint

WORKPLACE PRACTICE

This activity will give you practice at building self-esteem.

Suppose you are interested in a job as a messenger for the legal department of a book company. The company will require you to deliver important documents all over the city. You will need to know how to take transportation from one part of the city to another. It will be important for you to deliver the documents on time. You are going on an interview for the position.

A. Write the answers to the following questions on the lines.

1. The interviewer asks you why you would be the right person for the job. What do you say?

   _____

   _____

2. You know the public transportation system in your own neighborhood very well. You are not sure of the transportation system all over the city. What can you say to the interviewer?

   _____

   _____

3. The interviewer asks if you can be trusted with important documents. How do you convince the interviewer that you can?

   _____

   _____

4. The interviewer asks how you can make sure you are on time for work. What do you say?

   _____

   _____

B. Choose a partner.

5. Role-play this activity with a partner. Take turns being the interviewer and the job-seeker. Point out to each other when you are showing good self-esteem.

LESSON REVIEW

Key Words and Ideas

Draw a line from the word to its correct definition.

1. self-esteem   **a)** deserving, having value

2. worth   **b)** the opinion you have of yourself

Write the answers to the following questions on the lines.

3. What do people with good self-esteem think about themselves?

   _____

   _____

4. List two ways to help build your self-esteem.

   _____

   _____

Thinking About Having Self-Esteem

Circle the letter of the correct answer.

5. When you have good self-esteem you think that
   - **a)** you are always right.
   - **b)** you are doing your best.
   - **c)** no one else can do what you can do.
   - **d)** you never make mistakes.

6. One way to improve your self-esteem is to
   - **a)** draw up a plan to make changes.
   - **b)** have an opinion about yourself.
   - **c)** worry about your mistakes.
   - **d)** never make changes.

Workplace Workshop

7. Form a group with several classmates. Discuss the following questions:
   - **a)** How will good self-esteem help Tanya when she interviews for the job at Minton's Café?
   - **b)** How will good self-esteem help her if she gets the job?

LESSON 40
MOVING ON

Lesson Objectives

This lesson will help you answer these questions:

- **Why do people change jobs?**
- **What can you do when you want to change jobs?**

Words to Know:

promotion	a new job with more responsibility and more pay
revise	to change

Why People Change Jobs

Tanya had learned a lot at her job. Hank had given her a **promotion**. She got another raise and she was supervising two other workers. But Tanya felt ready to move on.

The job at Minton's Café would be a challenge for Tanya, but she felt prepared. She was ready for a change. She was ready to learn more. She was ready for new experiences.

Tanya was confident that she could handle the new job.

Here are some reasons people change jobs:

- for better working conditions and better benefits
- because of a life change—illness or a move to a new location
- to get more money or different hours
- for a better opportunity, or a chance to advance

Checkpoint

Why do people change jobs?

Think about your answer to this question. Write your answer on a separate piece of paper. Discuss your ideas with a partner and share them with the class.

When You Want to Change Jobs

You may feel ready to move on in the company you work for. If this is the case, keep the following things in mind:

- Discuss the possibility of a promotion with your supervisor. Explain why you think you deserve a promotion.

- If your supervisor does not agree, be polite. It is the supervisor's decision. You can ask again at a later date.

If you are interested in moving on to another company, here are some things to think about:

- Review Lesson 4, *Looking for Work*. Read again about networking, using want ads, and contacting companies.

- First speak to people you know. Do *not* discuss getting a new job with coworkers. They can be told at the time you get another job.

- **Revise** your résumé to bring it up-to-date.

- Review your interviewing skills.

JOB TIP

You may wish to write a short note of thanks to your supervisor after you leave a job. This may help you get a good reference.

Leaving the Job

Leave your old job in a professional way. Here's what you can do:

- Tell your supervisor about your new job. Don't say anything bad about the company you are leaving. Just say you're interested in new opportunities.

- Set a date when you will be leaving. This is usually two weeks from the day of your conversation. Your employer then will have some time to find another worker for your job.

- If you would like a reference from your supervisor, ask if that would be all right.

- Thank your supervisor for the good experience you have had working at the company.

- Try to leave on the best terms you can. You may run into these people again in the future.

What can you do when you want to change jobs?

Think about your answer to this question. Write your answer on a separate piece of paper. Discuss your ideas with a partner. Make a list and put it up on the bulletin board

Checkpoint

WORKPLACE PRACTICE

This activity will help you to understand about moving on to a new job.

A. Read the paragraph and answer the following questions on the lines.

Suppose you have worked as an assistant at a college snack bar for three years. Your salary is $20,000 a year. You live far from the school and do not like the long trip to work each day. You like the students, and you enjoy the work. The benefits are good, but you have little opportunity for a promotion. You are offered a job for a slightly lower salary at a bookstore three blocks from your house. The opportunities for advancement are good, but there are no benefits.

It's Not Always Easy

Think carefully about changing jobs. If you change jobs too often, an employer may not consider you for a job. Why would an employer not want to hire you?

1. What are the advantages of the old job?

_____

_____

2. What are the disadvantages of the old job?

_____

_____

3. What are the advantages of the new job?

_____

_____

4. What are the disadvantages of the new job?

_____

_____

5. If you take the new job, what will you say to your supervisor at the snack bar?

_____

_____

B. Choose a partner.

6. Discuss your answers with your partner.

LESSON REVIEW

Key Words and Ideas

Complete each sentence with a word from the box below.

promotion	revise

1. It's important to _____ your résumé before looking for a new job.

2. A _____ usually means more responsibility and more pay.

Write the answers to the following questions on the lines.

3. What are two reasons a person might change jobs?

   _____

   _____

4. If a supervisor asks why you are leaving for a new job, what should you say?

   _____

Thinking About Moving On

Circle the letter of the correct answer.

5. When you are looking for a new job, you should

   a) not tell your coworkers until you have a new job.

   b) tell everyone you know.

   c) use your old résumé.

6. When you leave your old job, you should

   a) say you're leaving in two days.

   b) be polite when you tell your supervisor you have a new job.

   c) tell your supervisor what was wrong with the job.

Workplace Workshop

7. You are ready to move on—from school to the workplace. With a group, talk about the ways in which you are now confident about this new stage of your life.

Unit 7 Review
B e i n g   S u c c e s s f u l

In this unit you learned about

- Feeling Sure of Yourself   • Moving On
- Building Self-Esteem

I. Vocabulary

Write the letter of the correct definition next to each word.

_____ 1. promotion   a) being sure that you can do
                                    something well

_____ 2. confident   b) a raise in rank and salary

_____ 3. worth   c) deserving, having value

Complete each sentence with a word from the box.

self-esteem   revise   positive attitude

4. Tanya knew she had to _____ her resume
   when she applied for the new job.

5. Maria had a _____ . She expected
   her fashion project to be a success.

6. Aldo's _____ was good. He knew he had
   done a fine job.

II. Main Ideas

Circle the letter of the correct answer.

7. You have good self-esteem when you

   a) respect yourself.   c) interrupt people.

   b) criticize others.

8. You can build self-esteem by

   a) making mistakes.   c) learning from mistakes.

   b) ignoring mistakes.

9. People who are confident

   a) know they can do a good job.

   b) are often nervous.

   c) don't manage their time well.

10. Employees like to hire people who

    a) do not need to learn anything.

    b) have a positive attitude.

    c) believe things do not turn out well.

11. A good reason to change jobs is to

    a) better your chances for advancement.

    b) have more stress.

    c) be with your friends.

12. When you appreciate your own worth, you

    a) know you're better than anyone else.

    b) think you cannot get another job.

    c) know that you can do a good job.

13. When you leave a job, you should tell your supervisor

    a) what was wrong with your old job.

    b) that you are leaving for new opportunities.

    c) that you will be gone in three days.

III. What Would You Do?

Write your answer to the following questions on the lines.

14. Suppose that you are a supervisor at the local grocery store. You just hired Greta to be a cashier. She doesn't feel sure of herself. What can you say to help her build her confidence?

    _____

    _____

15. You have been working at the local library for three years. At first, you felt you would never be able to do your job. Now you feel confident about being able to do your work. Describe how being confident helps you at your job.

    _____

    _____

16. Suppose that you work in a factory that makes stools. You are offered a new job at a another factory that makes chairs. You accept the job. Describe two things you might do before you leave for your new job.

    _____

    _____

IV. Solving Workplace Problems

Suppose you are a messenger for a movie studio. You want to be an assistant to the camera operator. You have taken courses on how to operate a camera in film school.

Write the answer to the following questions on the lines.

17. You think you deserve a chance to operate the camera. What do you say to your supervisor?

    _____

18. You get an interview with the person who heads the camera department. You want to explain that you have the knowledge for the job but you lack experience. What might you say during your interview to show that you are confident about your ability to perform the job?

    _____

    _____

19. You get the promotion! What do you say to your supervisor before you leave?

    _____

    _____

V. Unit Replay

Go back to the story on page 137. Reread it. Ask yourself again: How does it make you feel when you get better at doing things? Write your answer on a separate piece of paper.

VI. You . . . and Being Successful

Check ✔ the boxes next to the questions you can answer now.
Write an ✘ next to the ones you think you need to work on more.

☐ How does feeling sure of yourself help you at work? (Lesson 38)

☐ What is self-esteem? (Lesson 39)

☐ How can you build self-esteem? (Lesson 39)

☐ Why do people change jobs (Lesson 40)

☐ What can you do when you want to change jobs? (Lesson 40)

If you put an ✘ next to any question, go back and review the lesson.

A Final Note

Here's an update about the people involved in this book...

Anita decided that her main interest was hair styling. After looking for a few months, she accepted a job at Terry's Hair Salon. She likes the work there and is getting good experience.

Terrence started his job as a nurse's aide. At first, he worried about all the new things he had to do. But after a while he learned what he needs to know. He's now confident that he's doing a good job.

Ashley is doing well at the Hotel Statler. She was recently given a raise. At the annual company party, she received an award as "Employee of the Year." She was very proud!

Manuel has been working at Pete's Dry Cleaners for almost three years. Pete is opening a second store in town. He asked Manuel to be the assistant supervisor of the new store. Manuel was pleased with the promotion.

Ling got married and is having a baby. After the baby is born, she will leave her job for a few months. Then, she'll return to the Turner Building Supply Company. They'll be happy to have her back.

Dennis lost his job when the Barton Travel Agency closed. He spent a few months looking for another job. The Ryan Travel Company is now interested in hiring him. Dennis is thinking about their offer.

Tanya applied for the job at Minton's Café—and she got it. Hank was sorry to see her go, but he understood that it was a good opportunity. So far, Tanya likes her new job.

You too are about to look for a job. You've read these lessons. You've done the activities. You're ready to do a good job. You're ready for success!

Glossary

abbreviation a written word or phrase with several letters left out

abilities skills or talents for doing something

alphabetical order when items are listed in order of the letters of the alphabet: (a, b, c)

answering machine a machine that records telephone messages

apologize saying you're sorry

appreciate to be aware that something or someone is valuable

appropriate suitable at the time

assist to give help

atmosphere the mood of a place

attitude a way of acting that shows what someone is feeling or thinking

benefits extras offered by an employer. They can include health insurance, vacation time, education plans, and retirement plans

body language showing feelings using your body and your face

boundaries limits

casual clothes clothes worn when relaxing, such as around the house, at a picnic, or while playing

clients customers

common goal the end result that all team members work toward

communicate to share thoughts, feelings, and ideas with others

compromise a way to settle a conflict by having each side agree to give something up in order to get what each wants

concentrate pay close attention

confident being sure that you can do something well

conflicts disagreements

considerate thoughtful and caring about others

constructive criticism tips that help someone improve

contribute to play an important part

cooperate to work well with others

courtesy behaving in a way that shows good manners and respect for others

cover letter a letter that is sent with a résumé to introduce you to an employer

coworkers people you work with

criticize to find fault with something

deadline the date or time a task must be completed

discrimination the treatment of some people better than others for an unfair reason

diversity difference, variety

dress code rules for what to wear in a certain place, such as a job or restaurant

e-mail electronic mail by which messages can be sent by computer

employer the person or company who hires workers

employment agency a place that has listings of job openings

fax machine a machine that sends and receives information on paper using a phone line

feedback information people give you about your work

first impression what someone thinks about you after meeting you

flexible schedules working hours that are fixed to meet people's changing needs

goal something that you want and try to work toward

gossip to talk about people's personal lives

harassment the act of being annoyed again and again

hazards risks or dangers

income tax the money that everyone who works pays to the government

instructions orders about how to do something

international made up of people from different nations

Internet the system that connects millions of different kinds of computers around the world

laid off when workers lose their jobs because a company's needs have changed

long-term goal a goal that can be met in several months or a year

networking talking to people about jobs

on-line connected to a computer network

on-the-job training learning a job while working

organize arrange in a certain order

personal something that is private

personality all of a person's habits, behavior, and other qualities

positive attitude the expectation that things will turn out well

prejudice an opinion of other people that is not based on facts

pride feeling that you have importance

priority a level of importance

productive able to get a lot of work done

professional a person who acts in a responsible and businesslike way

promotion a new job with more responsibility and more pay

prompt on time

realistic within your reach

receipt a slip of paper that shows how much money was paid for something

records information that is saved

references people who know you well and will tell others you are a good worker

regret to be sorry for something

reliable able to be counted on and trusted

resources people and places that have useful information

résumé a summary of your education and work experience

revise to change

responsible doing what you are supposed to do

salary the amount of money a job pays

schedule a list of times to do things, a list of when things happen

self-esteem the opinion you have of yourself

severance pay extra money that an employer gives to laid-off workers

short-term goal a goal that can be met in several hours, days, or weeks

stress worry, strain, or pressure

success doing what you set out to do

supervisor someone who watches over and directs the work of another person

task work that needs to be done

technology the use of science to do practical things

thank-you note what you write to thank a person

threat an expression that hints that punishment or harm will follow

time sheet a sheet that lists the number of hours worked

tone a way of speaking that shows a certain feeling

trainee someone who is learning how to do a job

unemployment insurance government program that provides money to people who have lost their jobs

want ads advertisements placed by people who have jobs to fill

withholdings money that your employer takes from your paycheck for taxes

worth deserving, having value